THE LONG GAINERS

SIMS   *   FRANCIS
JEFFERSON   *   CAMPBELL

THE LONG GAINERS

SIMS ★ FRANCIS ★ JEFFERSON ★ CAMPBELL ★

BY BILL GUTMAN

tempo books
GROSSET & DUNLAP
A Filmways Company
Publishers • New York

Acknowledgments

The author would like to thank the following people for providing background material and information helpful in the preparation of this book: Joe Browne and Susan McCann of the National Football League; the Sports Information Departments of the University of Texas, Oregon University, Arizona State University, and the University of Oklahoma. Also, Dave Wintergrass of the New England Patriots, Rick Smith of the San Diego Chargers, and the public relations departments of the Houston Oilers and Detroit Lions. Thanks also to Don Weller, Personal Manager to Russ Francis, for his help in furnishing material dealing with Russ's life and career.

THE LONG GAINERS: SIMS, FRANCIS, JEFFERSON, CAMPBELL

Billy Sims

Rookies coming into the National Football League never have it easy. They are constantly under tremendous pressure—some to win starting jobs, others to live up to advance notices, and many simply to make the team. What's more, they usually have to undergo close personal scrutiny from the veterans to determine just what kind of fiber they're made of, and have to put up with their fair share of hazing, like singing their college songs, stuff like that.

When Billy Sims reported to the Detroit Lions training camp in the summer of 1980, he was well aware of what he'd be facing. At the team dinner that very first night, Billy was asked to make a short speech. Everyone watched in anticipation as he got up to speak.

"I'm Billy Sims from the University of Oklahoma," he said, with a straight face, "and I'm the reason most of you guys haven't gotten raises!"

The sound of instant laughter permeated the dining room. Billy Sims had broken the ice. There were also undoubtedly sighs of relief from the Lions' coaching staff. For Billy Sims was no ordinary rookie, and he wasn't in camp under ordinary circumstances. In fact, what Billy had said to his new teammates in a joking manner more than likely held a large measure of truth.

In 1980, Billy Sims was the number one choice of the entire National Football League, a running back expected to do for the Lions what the great Earl Campbell had done for the Houston Oilers some two years earlier. And it was no secret. In fact, New York Giants' coach Ray Perkins had described the 1980 college draft this way:

"It is in two parts—Billy Sims and then everybody else!"

Indeed, Billy had just completed an incredible career at the University of Oklahoma, a career that saw him win the Heisman Trophy as the best college player in the land, and he did that as a junior in 1978. He was an All-America once more his senior year and finished his Sooner career with 3,813 yards and an incredible, record-breaking average of 7.09 yards every time he carried the ball. He was considered to have pro potential to carry on the tradition of Jim Brown, Gale Sayers, O.J. Simpson, Walter Payton, Campbell, and the other truly great runners of the NFL.

But why did Billy claim he was the reason his teammates didn't get raises? Simply because in this era of big bucks, he had received perhaps the largest contract of any rookie ever coming into the league, a pact granted after months of bitter negotiations that not only made the Lions wonder if they'd lose him, but possibly threatened his relationship with coaches and teammates before training camp had even started.

So there was a touchy, maybe even explosive situation. Had Billy come strolling into camp, flashing gold chains and driving an expensive car, and playing the part of the high roller, he could have alienated a lot of people in a short amount of time. But those who thought this might happen didn't really know Billy Sims.

Sure, they knew him as a football player, a 6–0, 210-lb. slasher, with a tough, sure-footed running style that made him a genuine breakaway threat each time he carried the ball. But no one in Detroit really knew Billy Sims the man, that is, until he got there. Then they quickly found he was not a man you could dislike, or resent, even though his contract made him a millionaire.

For Billy Sims is an athlete and a competitor, a man who has paid his dues on the football field and in life. He's a man who knows what he wants, where his roots are, and the direction he wants his life to take when his playing days are over. He's also a man who has given himself freely to the fans and has done a great deal of work for the mentally retarded, his interest stemming from first-hand experience within his own family.

"What I like most about the game is the competition," Billy has said, "seeing how well I can do against other guys. Naturally, I don't like to lose, but if I feel I haven't done my best, winning isn't much fun, either."

Those are not the sentiments of a player who is willing to rest on his laurels and collect a big paycheck. He is also a person with a strong philosophy of life, whose ultimate direction points away from the excitement of the big city to the solitude of Hooks, Texas, where he spent a great deal of his childhood.

"I'll be going back there someday," Billy has said. "Football is just a game and you've got to stop playing games someday. But the land is real. I love to go home and get that feeling back, have that country atmosphere. And I love to see the old people there. That's where I get a lot of my strength from. I guess I'm just a country boy at heart."

But the country boy proved to be all football player once the bell rang. He came out smoking, gaining 153 yards in his first NFL game, and finishing the 1980 season with 1,303 yards on 313 carries. He also helped the Lions from a disastrous 2–14 mark in 1979 to a competitive 9–7 in 1980. And there are those who say Billy's season would have been even greater had the team not been hit by devastating injuries to its offensive line.

By the end of the year no one was complaining about Billy's contract or anything else, for that matter. He had proved to be every bit the football player he had been at Oklahoma, and at Hooks High School before that. And he was the kind of player who could be instrumental in turning a franchise around. Billy did this in spite of the tremendous pressure of being a number one draft choice, a former Heisman Trophy winner, and the bearer of that huge contract. But then again, Billy Sims has been overcoming long odds for most of his life.

Billy was actually born in St. Louis, Missouri, on September 18, 1955. His father's name was James Lomax and his mother had come to St. Louis from Hooks when she was married. But when Billy was just a few months old, they went back to Hooks, where most of his mother's family still lived.

Hooks, Texas, is a small town which then had a population of less than 2,500 people. It's located some two hours from Dallas and not all that far from the borders of Arkansas and Oklahoma. Billy has fond memories of his early years in Hooks, playing with all his relatives and always having friendly people around. But when he was about eight years old, the family moved back to St. Louis. By this time Billy had two brothers and two sisters, and things were decidedly more difficult.

In St. Louis, young Billy was back in a typical large inner city environment, and he didn't like it. If you weren't careful, you could find trouble around every streetcorner. As it is, he has memories of plenty of stealing going on, some of it involving friends, and even recalls people getting shot at in his general vicinity. He was still a young boy, but he already knew he hated the kind of life he saw there.

He did begin getting involved with sports during that time, but he played mostly basketball and soccer. Basketball, of course, has always been a big inner city game, and soccer has traditionally been a popular sport in the St. Louis area. But there wasn't much emphasis on football and Billy had no interest in it at all.

What he did have an interest in was getting out of St. Louis. The opportunity came when he was in the eighth grade, though the circumstances weren't happy ones. His parents had decided to separate. While the rest of the children remained in St. Louis with their mother, Billy knew he had to get out. He felt that strongly about it. The decision was made to let him return to Hooks and live with his grandmother, Sadie Sims.

Mrs. Sims lived alone, in a wooden house about four miles from the center of town. The house had been built by Billy's grandfather years earlier, so the family roots there ran deep. Billy would be living there with his grandmother and he soon decided to use her name. That's when he became Billy Sims.

The move was an obvious turning point in his life and he looks at it that way even today.

"Moving out of St. Louis and back to Hooks was a big factor in my life," he says. "I always liked the wide-open spaces and I left the inner city and its high crime rate. I just know if I hadn't made the change none of the good things would have happened to me."

As happy as Billy was to be back in Hooks, he knew he did not return to easy street. He explained it this way: "It was just my grandmother and me, and for the first time I had to carry my weight."

That meant working whenever he could at whatever jobs he could find. In the next few years he worked nights at a hospital, had a job in the school cafeteria, hauled hay for two cents a bale, chopped cotton for $1.50 a day, split wood, pumped gas, butchered hogs, and did a few other things. By the time he was 16, he was keeping things going at the old house down the dirt road.

"If I had a good, 84-hour week," Billy said, smiling, "I could make $120."

It was no laughing matter back then. Billy really had to work hard to keep himself and his grandmother above water. But whenever it got really hard and seemed they might not make it, he thought what it would have been like in St. Louis. That could only make him work harder. It was simply a case of considering the alternatives.

But life wasn't all work for Billy Sims then. When he was in the eighth grade he weighed just 130 pounds, but for the first time decided to play some football. His first inclination was to be a tackle or maybe a linebacker, but he was light for those positions and had the speed and natural moves best suited to running with the football.

Billy liked the game, and he kept playing in whatever spare time he had. He also enjoyed hunting and working on an old Chevy that he bought from a relative. Between school, football, work, and his other interests, there wasn't much time for hanging around. In fact, his hours at the Conoco Service Station, his main job after he turned 16, were 6 a.m. to 6 p.m. on weekends, and seven days a week in the summer.

By the time he reached Hooks High as a sophomore in 1972, he was already quite a player. Of course, playing for a small school in a little town tucked in the corner of Texas, Billy wasn't about to become an overnight sensation. In fact, Jack Coleman, the coach at Hooks High, had seen Billy play as an eighth grader, but still didn't know what kind of player he'd be getting.

"I knew he had ability," Coleman recalls, "but you can't really tell when they're in junior high how good they're going to be later."

Yet when Billy went out for football as a Hooks sophomore two years later, Coach Coleman knew he had himself a super runner. He made Billy a starter and let him loose on the rest of the schools in the area. Billy was nearly six feet by then, and filling out, though he still wasn't close to his present weight of 210 pounds. But he had all the other ingredients, the speed, the growing power, the ability to cut sharply and the instinct to do it at just the right moments. And he was tough.

Game after game Billy ripped off the yardage. With each passing weekend, people watched in amazement as he romped all over the field, eluding and overpowering bigger players. Little did most of them know, had it not been for Billy's own persistence, he might have been spending his Friday nights on the street corners of St. Louis instead of running wild for the Hooks Hornets.

Billy's poorest game as a sophomore saw him gain 123 yards. That was his *poorest* game. In fact, it would be the poorest game of the thirty-eight contests he played in during his high school career. He had a number of 200 yard games that season, and was, in effect, just giving people a preview of things to come.

By his junior year more people were pouring out to see this marvelous running back, and Billy didn't disappoint them. There were outstanding games that year, and anything less than 200 yards began to look like an off day. And by then, his coach couldn't say enough about him.

"He's the best running back I've ever been around," said Jack Coleman. "A lot of it is natural ability. Billy has good strength, speed, and size. But besides that, he works darn hard at it. He's just a good all-around kid."

In a regional playoff game against Rockwell High that year, Billy's play defied description. He simply ran wild, was unstoppable all afternoon. He broke tackle after tackle, faked defenders, burst through holes that didn't seem to exist. When the game ended, he had rolled up a fantastic 381 yards and had scored six touchdowns! And he did this despite the fact that the Rockwell defense knew he was coming. By then, the Hooks offensive playbook simply read: Sims-left, Sims-right, Sims-up-the-middle.

Even though Hooks played in a double-A conference, due to the small size of the school (triple-A was considered the best), his accomplishments could no longer be ignored. Area college coaches began getting films of the Hooks games and marveling at the junior running back. One of those who received a film of the sensational Rockwell game was Barry Switzer, the head coach at the University of Oklahoma. Billy's junior year at Hooks was also Switzer's first at Oklahoma, and the coach was determined to continue the great Sooner winning tradition. He recalls seeing the films of Billy for the first time.

"I knew Hooks had to be a small school because I had never heard of it before," Switzer recalls. "But how could I ignore this kid running for nearly 400 yards and looking great every time he got the ball. So I called his coach, Jack Coleman, and asked if it would be possible to talk with Billy. He said Billy was right there and put him on. I guess you could say that's when I started recruiting him."

Other schools began coming after him, also, especially when he looked better than ever at the beginning of his senior year. Yet Billy was taking everything in stride. He still worked very hard at the Conoco station and other jobs, enjoyed working on and driving his old Chevy, and he had met a girl. Her name was Brenda and she was a cheerleader at rival New Boston High. They began going steady that summer and would be married some four years later when they were both students at Oklahoma.

At the beginning of his senior year, the 1974 season, Billy looked better than ever. Once again he gobbled up the yards in great chunks. His standard seemed to be the 200-yard game, rather than 100. And he had another 300-yarder, getting 314 against Winsboro High. More colleges were now interested in him, but Oklahoma continued to make a major effort. In fact, Coach Switzer sent one of his assistants, Bill Shimek, to Hooks, with orders to hang around until Billy decided. Shimek took a room in a motel in Texarkana and stayed for the better part of two months.

"I'll never forget the first time I saw Billy," recalls Shimek. "He was carrying two big buckets of cow feed just like they were water glasses. From the waist up he looked like a Greek God. He only weighed about 180 pounds then, but I thought, 'Lordy, he's something.' "

As the Hooks season wore on, Billy went over the 1,000-yard mark, then the 2,000-yard mark, and headed for 3,000, an almost incomprehensible figure. And the scouts and recruiters continued coming to Hooks. It was hard for Billy in that he didn't have a father or older brother to approach for advice. Fortunately, he got some solid guidance from his coach.

"Coach Coleman was a big help to me then," says Billy. "He was a terrific guy and he knew enough not to tell me which college to attend. He just helped me handle the recruiters, pointed out some things he felt I should know, and let me make up my own mind."

Coach Switzer at Oklahoma was also keeping close tabs on Billy. He spoke with Bill Shimek often and, knowing that Billy's games were on Friday night, would sometimes call him at the Conoco station on Saturday, usually before his own Sooners would go into action. One time, he called Billy a little later than usual.

"We were playing Colorado at Boulder," says Coach Switzer, "and by halftime it was something like 28 or 35 to nothing. So when we came into the lockerroom there wasn't much I had to say. I happened to notice a pay phone on the wall and said to myself it was a good time to call Billy. So I spent the halftime of the Colorado game talking to Billy Sims."

For Billy's part, he was beginning to lean toward Oklahoma. The school wasn't that far from home, and they had a great winning tradition. Plus they usually ran the ball as well as anyone. It was a place where an outstanding back could really shine.

That's just what Billy continued to do at Hooks. In fact, when the season ended, he had completed one of the most incredible high school careers ever. In 38 games, he rushed for 7,738 yards, getting over 3,000 of them as a senior. He carried the ball 1,128 times for an average of 6.9 yards a carry, and he averaged a shade over 203 yards for those 38 games. In addition, he scored 78 touchdowns and 48 extra points for 615 points.

He was over 100 yards every time out (the 123 yards early in his sophomore year was his low), went for more than 200 yards on 18 occasions, and was over the 300-yard barrier twice. At that time it was the second greatest high school running record in American high school history.

"I've never seen anybody like him," said Johnny Green, who was sports editor of the nearby *Texarkana Gazette*. "What impressed me the most was the playoff games both his junior and senior years. He played on bad legs both years and was over 200 yards in all the games. I remember him having two bad knees in a game against Bowie and he still got 237 yards."

Coach Coleman recalled similar performances. "He was injured to one degree or another all of his senior year," said the coach. "Not serious injuries, but sometimes enough to slow a man up. Not Billy, he played as if he was one hundred percent. And he was always a team player in spite of his individual success. Never had any problems with him whatsoever."

Because he had always worked so hard to support his grandmother and himself, Billy never had time to follow college or even professional football. One time, when someone asked him if he had an idol, he laughed and said, yes, himself. So there were no preferences when he began looking at schools. But he had always liked the extra attention paid him by Oklahoma. And when he went to visit the campus at Norman, things were pretty much decided.

"Once I got up there, everyone made me feel right at home," Billy said. "I just felt there were a lot of nice people there and it would be a good place for me. Before I left to return home, I had already made up my mind that that's where I wanted to go."

Of course, there is tremendous pressure on high school stars of Billy's magnitude. If not protected somehow, recruiters and coaches can practically jump out of the trees to get a word in for their schools. The phone can ring at any hour, day or night, and people can come to the door demanding entrance to the family home. So with Billy on the brink of making his decision and recruiters still trying to sell their own programs, he returned from Oklahoma and disappeared. No one could find him.

"The rumors were really flying," said Johnny Green, the sports editor. "Some people thought he went up to New Boston where his girl friend lived.

But others thought Oklahoma was hiding him, so no one else could make a last minute pitch. Yet at the same time, Bill Shimek from Oklahoma looked as worried as everyone else. He didn't know where Billy was, either."

A few days later Billy returned, and promptly announced to all that he would be attending the University of Oklahoma in the fall of 1975. Then he ended the mystery by explained where he had been.

"I had already made up my mind to go to Oklahoma," he said, "but I knew there were going to be a whole lot of coaches in Hooks the next few days trying to change my mind. I just didn't want to see them, so I went to St. Louis to visit my mother for a while."

It was finally settled. In June, Billy graduated from Hooks High, being named *Mr. Hooks High* by the 110 seniors in his class. He wasn't about to rest on his laurels. He had continued to work hard throughout the school year at the Conoco station and with his other jobs. For the summer, he had a construction job in Texarkana which he figured would help build him up for his first year of football at Oklahoma. He wanted to be ready.

"I think I have a good chance to start this year," he said, "but if I don't it won't be a big letdown. After all, it's just my first year."

Billy wasn't kidding when he told someone that he wanted to play with the best. The Oklahoma Sooners had a great winning tradition. They had been playing competitively since 1895, and had come into national prominence during the coaching reign of Bud Wilkinson, who was head man from 1947 to 1963. During that time Wilkinson teams won 145 games, lost just 29, and tied four, being acclaimed national champions on three occasions.

During an incredible eleven-year stretch from 1948 through 1958, Wilkinson's Sooner teams compiled an almost unbelievable mark of 107–8–2, including four undefeated, untied seasons. There was a brief down period after Wilkinson retired, but the team revived under Chuck Fairbanks, who coached from 1967 to 1972. When Fairbanks left for the pros, Barry Switzer took over. He had been an assistant at OU since 1966. In his first year as head man the team went 10–0–1 and were ranked third in the country.

Then in 1974 they won all eleven of their games and were named national champions once again. The team led the nation in total offense, averaging 507.7 yards a game, in rushing with 438.8 yards a game, and in scoring with 43 points per contest. That was the team Billy Sims was joining in 1975, and why he said he was going to play with the best.

There were some eight All-Americans on the 1974 Sooner squad, including running back Joe Washington, who had rambled for 1,321 yards, and who would be back for his senior year in '75. In fact, Washington was just the latest in a series of great runners who had become stars at the Norman, Oklahoma campus. And many of them had gone on to become equally fine professional players.

The first of the great ones was probably Billy Vessels in the early 1950s. Then in the mid-50s along came Tommy McDonald and Clendon Thomas. The unpredictable Joe Don Looney flared briefly but brightly in 1962, and was followed by steady Jim Grisham. In the late 1960s came rugged workhorse Steve Owens, and he was followed in the early '70s by speedy Greg Pruitt, still a star with the Cleveland Browns.

Joe Washington came in during Pruitt's final year, and now Billy was coming in as Washington prepared for his final campaign. So the stage was set for Billy Sims to become the next great Sooner running back. The question was, could he do it? He wouldn't have the stage to himself. There were some other fine runners at Norman, including Elvis Peacock and Kenny King. So Billy wouldn't be starting automatically.

He was also joining a team that had more than fine running backs. The defense was also studded with All-Americans. Linebacker Rod Shoate and safety Randy Hughes had graduated in '74, but returning were Lee Roy and Dewey Selmon, familiar names to pro fans today. They were joined by other fine defenders. The offense ran from the wishbone formation, a fast-paced running formation that saw the quarterback run more often than he passed. In 1975 the Sooners had a fine QB in Steve Davis. The team fully expected to be formidable once more.

So Billy came to Oklahoma filled with optimism and great expectations. He was there a bit more than a month and already working hard at football when he received a devastating blow. His beloved grandmother, Sadie, whom he had lived with and worked so hard for, died of cancer. Billy hadn't known she was so ill, or, as he said, "I never would have left home." Perhaps it was the final unselfish thing his grandmother did for him, concealing her illness enough so that he would go to college.

That spurred him to work even harder. But as the season approached, he found himself running behind All-American Washington on the Sooner depth chart. And when the 1975 season opened, Billy wasn't playing. The team had just too many experienced runners ahead of him.

It was another memorable season for the Sooners. They won some big (62–7 over Oregon, 46–10 against Pittsburgh), and some close (21–20 over Colorado, 28–27 versus Missouri), and some in between. There was only one stumbling block, a 23–3 upset loss to Kansas. But when they won the Orange Bowl game against Michigan, 14–6, the team finished with an 11–1 record and were acclaimed national champions once again.

The only problem for Billy was that he hardly played. He shared in the joy of winning the national title, but didn't feel he contributed very much to it. He had just fifteen carries from scrimmage and gained 95 yards, not a very busy workload during a twelve-game schedule. He did give a slight hint of things to come by averaging 6.3 yards per carry, but in the entire scheme of things, it wasn't very much.

Outwardly, Billy seemed to take it well. "I was honored to be playing behind as great a runner as Joe Washington," he said. But he admitted to friends that it was a discouraging season for him. And he couldn't be sure about the future.

"They had running backs running out their ears," was the way he put it. "Some of them were big names and I was just a little freshman from Hooks, Texas."

Washington had graduated in 1976, and Billy was again in a battle for a starting position. The Sooners were looking to another big year and Billy was hoping to make a greater contribution. As the season opened, Coach Switzer was rotating his many fine backs. It was obvious that the runners who did the best in the early going would get the bulk of the playing time.

The club opened against Vanderbilt that year and Billy looked confident the first couple of times he carried the ball. He had one nifty run and after three carries had already gained 44 yards for a 14.6 average. Little did anyone know it, but they would be Billy's only three carries of the year. Shortly after it was revealed that he had left the field with a shoulder injury. It was diagnosed as a cracked and separated shoulder. He would be out for quite some time.

Since the club was very deep at running back, it was soon decided to redshirt Billy for the entire season. That meant if he was taken off the roster immediately, the season wouldn't count for him and he'd have an extra year of eligibility, in effect, a fifth season. The Sooner coaching staff thought this was a better way then to let him return for the final few games, which would add up to pretty much a lost season anyway. It was sound thinking, but the whole thing was very depressing to Billy. It would be difficult for any athlete, especially one who had known such overwhelming success during his three years of high school.

"When I injured the shoulder I really thought that maybe it was time I gave up football," Billy admits. "I felt that the body could take only so much punishment and maybe mine had had enough. I certainly had my share of bumps and bruises in high school."

So Billy was really down and perhaps for the only time in his career thinking of packing it all in. The thing that stopped him was the memory of the grandmother, who had already done so much for him when she was alive.

"I knew she wouldn't have approved of me quitting," he said, "and I always wanted to make her proud of me. So I was determined to stick it out."

Once the injury healed, Billy was allowed to practice with the team, but couldn't suit up for the games. The way he initially described it was "starting from the bottom again, holding dummies and being hit." But as weeks past, he began to find a very positive result out of the redshirt experience.

"I thought redshirting was terrible at first," he said, "but I soon began realizing it was like an extra year of training. Once I was completely well, I worked out with the team every day. I had to be what they call The Dummy. That meant I would run all the opponents' plays in practice each week. It was a drill meant to get our defense ready to face a certain kind of offense, I'm sure it made the defense better, but I *know* it made me better. I suddenly realized that the defense rarely got a good shot at me. I was doing a lot of good things and my confidence not only returned, it grew."

Without Billy, the team had another fine year, finishing at 9–2–1. So when 1977 arrived, the club was still very strong and Billy was officially a sophomore for the second time. Only now it looked as if he'd finally get his chance to show his stuff. In the opener against Vanderbilt, Billy was seeing a lot of action and playing well. But late in the game, the Sooners were behind when, despite his injuries of the past year, Billy really put his body on the line. Coach Switzer remembers:

"Billy got us back in it with a couple of real hurdling acts," the coach said. "He got us a first down in a key situation when he went airborne for five yards on a fourth-and-one play. He also hurdled into the end zone from the seven yard line, one of the damndest things I'd ever seen. The seven-yard line was where his feet left the ground and he landed in the end zone. He just ran full speed and leapt. Came down for six and no one ever touched him."

The Sooners won the game, 25–23, and Billy was happy. For the first time he really felt a part of the team. It continued that way for the next two weeks. But in the third game the injury jinx struck again. He hurt his right ankle and was on the shelf once more. This time it wasn't a totally disabling injury, but bad enough to limit his effectiveness and make him a part time player once again. The net result, 406 yards on 65 carries for a 6.2 average. It was his best effort yet, but in view of his expectations, very disappointing. The team was 10–2, but for three years Billy had just 545 yards on 83 carries and he really began wondering if his time would ever come.

Then came 1978, and by then all Billy's accomplishments at Hooks High were basically ancient history. And because of his various injuries, not that much was expected from him. In fact, his picture wasn't included on the cover of the 1978 Sooner media guide which featured the team's "all-stars." Yet during the preseason, Billy was looking great and when the season was ready to begin, he was in the starting backfield with quarterback Thomas Lott, fullback Kenny King, and halfback David Overstreet. They were still running the wishbone.

The Sooners traveled to Palo Alto, California, to open the season against Stanford, a team that liked to put the ball in the air. Billy started the scoring with a two-yard TD run and helped the Sooners to a 28–10 halftime lead. But Stanford battled back to make it 28–20 at the end of three. In the fourth period the Sooners began driving again. With the ball on the Sooner 46, Billy took a pitchout from QB Lott and swung around end. He juked an end and cut back beautifully, sprinting 27 yards to the 19.

His run set up the final Sooner TD, which proved to be the winner as Oklahoma held off a late Stanford rally to win, 35–29. Quarterback Lott got most of the press, tossing touchdown passes of 70 and 17 yards, and scoring twice himself, once on a 19-yard run. But Billy had come through his first real test very well, gaining 107 yards on 19 carries. If he could only stay healthy, this could be the year he would finally put it all together.

The next two weeks were both laughers, as the Sooner steamroller crushed West Virginia, 52–10, and Rice, 66–7. Coach Switzer used the games to get a look at his second stringers and to protect his top stars. Billy played only about a quarter in each game, yet still gained 114 yards on just eight carries against West Virginia. He also scored on a beautiful 41-yard burst. Against Rice, he had just 33 yards in eight tries, but again scored the first TD of the game, this time from 11 yards out. Now came a real tough one against the Tigers of Missouri.

Early in the opening session the Sooners worked the ball to the Missouri 42. Billy took a pitchout and was off to the races, sliding past tacklers, faking others, and outrunning the rest, all the way to the end zone for the game's first score. Later in the session he got the ball again, this time at midfield. Once again he did his thing, sprinting 50 yards to paydirt. The Sooner machine was in high gear and Billy Sims was finally becoming the biggest cog in the wheel.

It was an outstanding offensive display by the

entire club and Billy was showing all the
dimensions of his game. In the third period he
threw a crushing block that sprung halfback David
Overstreet on a 64-yard TD romp. The final score
was 45–23, and Billy had his greatest game as a
Sooner, gaining 166 yards on 14 carries, scoring
four times along the way. Overstreet had 153 yards
on ten carries, so the Sooner ground attack was
really devastating.

For his efforts, Billy was named Big Eight Conference Offensive Player of the Week. Slowly, he
was beginning to get recognition. But perhaps the
most important thing was that he was healthy, and
keeping his fingers crossed. But he couldn't rest on
his laurels. The Sooners now had to travel to Dallas to meet archrival and always tough Texas.

In the previous four games, Billy had scored the
first touchdown. In the Texas game, he did even
better. He got the first two scores, going in from 18
yards out and then one yard out. It was a 17–3 game
at the half, and the Sooners went on to win, 31–10.
Billy gained a tough 131 yards on 25 carries, threw
another wicked block to spring Overstreet for a
score, and caught a 35-yard pass from Thomas
Lott. It was the first pass thrown his way all year
and he grabbed it with ease. He was suddenly
blossoming into a full-fledged star.

The next week the club won a squeaker, getting
by a sky-high Kansas team, 17–16. But Billy was
getting better. He rambled for 192 yards on 30 carries. He was proving quite durable, surviving 55
carries in his last two games. What more, he was a
threat to go the distance every time he touched the
ball.

Oklahoma won its next three games easily, whipping Iowa State, Kansas State, and Colorado. But

that wasn't the big news. Save that for Billy Sims. He tied an NCAA record by rushing for more than 200 yards in all three games. Now football fans all over the country began to hear about the super runner from Oklahoma.

Against Iowa State he ran for 231 yards on 20 carries, including jaunts of 63 and 53 yards. He was Big Eight Offensive Player of the Week, made the UPI National Backfield of the Week, and was the AP Co-Offensive Player of the Week. Then against Kansas State he got 202 yards on 25 tries and was tabbed *Sports Illustrated* Magazine and Associated Press Offensive Player of the Week.

He capped it with a 221-yard performance against Colorado, carrying another 25 times, including a brilliant 59-yard run. Once again he was Big Eight Offensive Player of the Week and on the UPI Backfield of the Week. The Sooners had won nine straight and were strong candidates to take another national championship. And for the first time, people were beginning to call Billy Sims a candidate for the Heisman Trophy, given annually to the man judged the best college player in the land. One man who didn't think he had a chance was Billy Sims.

"I'm just not well known enough to win," he said. "I had no preseason buildup like some of the others. And I think it will go to a senior, someone like Rich Leach, the quarterback for Michigan. Plenty of people are still saying, 'Who's Billy Sims?'"

Billy was right about a couple of things. The Heisman usually goes to a glamour player, a quarterback or runner, and one who is well known, just missed the year before, and who is heavily promoted by his school. The promotion begins even

before the season, and since Billy was such an unknown quantity, there was no buildup for him.

But he couldn't think too much about that. The
Sooners had to hit the road for a crucial meeting
with the Nebraska Cornhuskers, another outstanding team and a club just a game behind Oklahoma
in the Big Eight race.

The Sooners scored first in the opening period
and they did it the usual way. Billy rambled 44
yards into the end zone and the extra point made it
a 7–0 game. Then in the second period, the Cornhuskers came back to tie it and the half ended with
the game deadlocked at 7–7.

Nebraska took a 14–7 lead in the third period, but
Billy capped another Sooner drive by running in
from thirty yards out. The game was tied once
again. Oklahoma might have held the lead, but
they were fumbling away chances all afternoon.
Then midway through the final session, Nebraska
scored on a 24-yard field goal. They had a 17–14
lead, which marked the first time all year that the
Sooners had trailed in a ballgame. Then, with time
running out, Oklahoma started what could be their
final drive for a victory.

With Billy doing the bulk of the work, the
Sooners moved to the Cornhusker 20. Once again,
quarterback Lott gave the ball to Sims, and Billy
dashed around the right side. He broke one tackle,
then another, still another, and a fourth, with an
incredibly tough, gutty run. For a second it looked
as if he might go all the way. But he was hit again
at the three-yard line . . . and the ball squirted out
of his hands. Nebraska recovered! Billy's fumble
had killed the drive and the Cornhuskers then ran
out the clock to preserve their victory.

It was a bitter defeat for the Sooners and especially for Billy Sims. Not only did it all but end Oklahoma's chances for a sixth national title, but it also dropped them into a first place tie in the Big Eight with the Cornhuskers. In addition, the game was on national television, so Billy's fumble, one of nine Sooner bobbles that afternoon, was seen by a multitude of fans. And unfortunately, more people would remember the fumble than the fine, 153-yard day Billy had. He also felt the fumble ended even the most remote chance that he might win the Heisman.

The club rebounded the final game, rolling over Oklahoma State, 62–7. As usual, Billy scored the first TD of the game, then three more as he rambled for 209 yards on 30 carries. It didn't wipe out the memory of the Nebraska fumble, but it sure helped ease it a bit. The team finished the regular season with a 10–1 mark and Billy Sims had put together one of the greatest seasons in NCAA history.

He finished the regular season with 1,762 yards on 231 carries for an incredible average of 7.6 yards a pop, and he scored 20 touchdowns. The TD's and average gain were tops in the nation, as was his 160.2 per-game rushing average. There was little doubt that he was a player who had come from nowhere to status of consensus All-American.

Billy was overjoyed at the way things had turned out. "I looked at this as just a survival year," he said. "I just wanted to come out walking after the last two years. I guess it turned out a little better than that."

Others were even more enthusiastic. "He's got to be the best back in the country," said his coach, Barry Switzer. "He's certainly as good as any back who's played at Oklahoma since I've been here.

And when you take guys like Greg Pruitt, Steve Owens, Joe Washington, Horace Ivory, Elvis Peacock, you know we haven't had many ordinary backs.

"You see so many good ones and you keep saying there can't be anyone better. But Billy probably has more talent than all of those guys. He's big, strong, fast, elusive, breaks tackles, and is stronger than the other guys we've had here. I guess I'd describe him as a snaky runner. He snakes and slithers through people and yet he's so strong he can break tackles."

Switzer had plenty of people agreeing with him. Right after the season ended, the honors began pouring in. Billy was named to all the major All-America teams. He was also named Big Eight Offensive Player of the Year, and the AP and UPI Player of the Year. He was also *Sport* Magazine's Player of the Year. In fact, it seemed as if he was everyone's Player of the Year.

Then in December came the news everyone was waiting for. Billy Sims was named the winner of the Heisman Trophy, the third Oklahoma player to win it and only the sixth junior to take the coveted prize. He had beaten out Penn State quarterback Chuck Fusina in a close vote, 827 points to 750. In fact, Fusina got more first place votes, 163-151, but Billy scored more consistently in all six voting regions of the country.

"I really didn't expect it," Billy said. "I thought I'd be in the race, but I always thought Rich Leach would win. He was a starter for four years, and I'm just a junior. I thought that would work against me."

Right away people began asking if Billy thought he could win it again the following year. After all, only one player, Archie Griffin of Ohio State, had won it two years in a row.

"It's possible," Billy said, "but there are so many factors, so many things to consider. I've got to stay healthy all year and have solid support from my teammates. If I play well and the team plays well, then I have a chance."

There was one thing that made it all sweeter. Billy's roommate and friend, Greg Roberts, a Sooner guard, won the Outland Trophy as the nation's best lineman. So the two friends really cornered the market on the top hardware.

But there was still another game to play. Billy led the Sooners onto the field at the Orange Bowl on New Year's Day. There, they got revenge on Nebraska, beating their Big Eight rivals, 31–24, as Billy made up for his fumble during the regular season by having a brilliant game and being named Most Valuable Player.

Billy was more than a football player at Oklahoma. Once the season ended he studied, making up for lost time during football. His major was recreational therapy and he spent three days a week working with the Oklahoma Association for Retarded Citizens. There was a personal reason for Billy's interest in this kind of work, something he has continued right to the present.

"I've got a fifteen-year-old brother who is retarded," Billy said at the time. "That's how I got into it. And it's not always easy. You've got to have a strong heart for that kind of work."

For the first time since his high school days Billy was again a celebrity. Only this time it was on a much larger scale. During the off-season, the summer months, he ran and lifted weights with teammate David Overstreet, and he sold ads for the

Oklahoma Sooner Weekly. And as the Heisman Trophy winner and local hero, there were plenty of people willing to buy ads from him. It was a good summer, but as the new season approached, Billy found himself anxious to go again. The demands on his time were beginning to get to him.

"Right now I'm just about laid out," he said, toward the end of the summer. "I'm just trying to stay home and get some rest. But it's tough. People keep calling me at all hours. They want all kinds of things—tickets, autographs, speak here, speak there, do this, do that. The fans around here are really something."

To many, the Sooners did not have the same kind of powerhouse team they had fielded a year earlier. But they were still formidable, and they still had Billy Sims. And accordingly, people were expecting a great deal from the Heisman Trophy winner. In some cases, they were even expecting miracles.

The team opened against Iowa in what was supposed to be an easy game. But the Hawkeyes took a 6–0 lead as the Sooners blew several chances. Billy finally scored on a one-yard run in the second period giving his club a 7–6 halftime advantage. In the fourth period Billy and quarterback J.C. Watts each scored and the final was 21–6, with Billy getting 106 yards.

Next came an easy, 49–13 victory over Tulsa, as Billy scored two more and was over 100 yards again. A week later the steamroller returned, 63–21, over Rice, as Billy had 103 yards on just 12 carries in one-half of play. A week later he got 118 yards and scored four times as the Sooners whipped Colorado, 49–24.

The Sooners had won four straight and Billy was

obviously still the main man. But instead of getting 175–200 yards, he was in the low 100s, and because of the expectations, that wasn't enough. Some people began to infer that Billy wasn't playing up to his 1978 form, that maybe his blocking was better the year before and he wasn't the standout he was thought to be. More and more attention was being focused on Charles White, the tailback for the University of Southern California. White was a smallish, but durable back who was already the all-time USC rusher and had finished fourth in the Heisman balloting a year earlier. Now, he was being talked about as the runner of 1979.

Then came the team's first big game, against Texas at Dallas, and it just wasn't the Sooner's day. The Longhorn defense dominated all afternoon and Texas won a hardfought, 16–7, victory. As for Billy, he failed to gain 100 yards for the first time in fourteen games. So while he had averaged some 160 yards a game in '78, after five games in 1979, he was averaging just over 100 per game. There was little doubt now that he wasn't the same explosive player he had been the year before.

A week later the Sooners returned to winning ways with a 38–6 victory over Kansas State. But Billy, nursing sore ribs from the Texas game, managed just 67 yards. The superstar of '78 was quickly becoming just another good back in '79.

"I don't agree with that," said one Oklahoma newsman, who had covered the Sooners for some time. "There's nothing wrong with Billy Sims. The club has had some real easy games and he did run into a buzzsaw in the Texas defense. But there are also other guys who can play and Billy isn't a one-man team. I'm betting that when the chips are down and before the year is out, Billy will be the same galloper everyone raved about last year. A lot of people don't realize it, but this game is more than numbers and stats. Billy Sims is a complete player."

A week later, Billy proved the man right. His number was called more often and he responded with a 202-yard day and four touchdowns, as the Sooners rolled over Iowa State, 38–9. He also showed a fine pair of hands in grabbing a 42-yard pass from quarterback J.C. Watts. Billy was rarely used as a pass receiver, but when they called on him, he was there.

Two more very easy victories followed, Oklahoma State bowing, 38–7, and Kansas falling, 38–0. Billy scored four times against Oklahoma State, but did not have overwhelming stats, and rushed for just 128 yards against Kansas. But again, the team didn't need any more from him to win handily, so he couldn't be faulted. Yet because of all these factors, it was pretty much conceded that he wouldn't be repeating as the Heisman winner.

Then came Missouri and this one was a real dogfight. The Tigers scored first on a 39-yard field goal before David Overstreet scored from the two, giving the Sooners a 7–3 lead. But the Tigers scored in the second period, missing the point after, but taking a 9–7 lead into the lockerroom at halftime. The only bright spot was Billy, who was eating up the yardage all half, though the Tiger defense stopped the Sooners in key situations.

Then at the outset of the third period, Billy broke through. He took a pitchout and raced 70 yards for an Oklahoma score. The kick gave the Sooners a 14–9 lead. A Watts score made it 21–9, but the Tigers battled back, making it 21–16 at the end of three. The fourth period was another pitched battle and the Sooners prevailed, 24–22.

As for Billy, he had finally silenced the critics. He broke loose for a career high 282 yards on 36 rugged carries and was named *Sports Illustrated* and Big Eight Back of the Week. With the season down to a final game, he couldn't have picked a better time to get hot.

The finale would be against Nebraska, and once again it would be for the Big Eight title since both clubs were unbeaten in conference play. The Cornhusker defense had given up just 67.2 rushing yards per game all year. And they'd be geared to stop Billy Sims. Sooner Coach Switzer noted just what a tough game this would be.

"We haven't played close to our offensive potential this year," he said, "and our defense clearly isn't as strong. We just don't have as many good players, and we're more likely to make mistakes than they are. Last season I thought we were the best team. This year Nebraska is."

Billy still hadn't completely forgotten his crucial fumble in the Nebraska game the year before, and as he later said, "It was the first game all season I'd really been pumped up for." He had also told Switzer days before the game, "Coach, I'll get this one."

Midway through the first period he gave an indication of things to come. The ball was on the Sooner 32 when Billy took it off right tackle. A couple of his smooth moves and he was in the clear, racing 68 yards for an apparent score. But no. A flag was down. A clipping penalty called the TD back, but Billy still got credit for a 53-yard scamper. Then the Cornhusker defense stiffened, and at the end of one it was a scoreless tie.

Billy's running set up a Sooner field goal in the

second period, but Nebraska came back to score a touchdown and take a 7–3 lead into the lockerroom. No one could fault Billy, however. In the first quarter alone he had run for 113 yards! He was on his way to another great game. In fact, after the first quarter, Nebraska coach Tom Osborne said: "I didn't think he could gain that many on us."

Early in the third period quarterback J.C. Watts took over. He hit tight end Forrest Valora for a 58-yard TD and the kick gave the Sooners a 10–7 lead. Then early in the final period came the big play of the game. And it was pulled off by Billy Sims.

With the ball on the Sooner 21, Billy burst off left tackle. He popped through one tackle, juked a linebacker and was off to the races. Only the Nebraska safetyman prevented him from going all the way, angling him out of bounds at the eight. Four plays later quarterback Watts scored the decisive touchdown. A late Nebraska score made the final 17–14. The Sooners had taken the Big Eight and were off to the Orange Bowl once again.

Billy's 71-yard gallop in the final session capped off a brilliant 247-yard day on 28 carries in his final regular season game. In the first nine games, Billy had gained 977 yards, but in the final pair, he had run for another 529, giving him 1,506 yards for the season on 224 carries for another fine, 6.7, average. He also scored 22 touchdowns, two better than the previous year. It had taken a while, but the raves were back.

"I asked myself how Sims could miss getting the Heisman again," said Coach Switzer, after the game. "I think I know the answer. It's because people have made him out to be some kind of superman. They expect him to rush for 200 yards every game, forgetting that 100 yards is a great, great day for anyone. And Billy makes it look too easy. He makes a great play almost look routine. There will never be another player like him at Oklahoma."

Quarterback Watts put it in simpler terms: "When Billy gets into the secondary, it's a nightmare for them."

Of course, Billy was everybody's All-American for a second year, only this time he didn't win the Heisman. As expected, the prize went to USC's Charles White, who put together a great season to become college football's second all-time ground gainer. But Heisman or not, the pro people still considered Billy far and away the best prospect coming out of the college ranks in 1979. And he was a close second to White in the Heisman voting, at that.

Billy finished his regular season career at Oklahoma with 3,813 yards on 538 carries. He had an amazing average of 7.09 yards per carry for his career and he also scored 50 touchdowns. You couldn't ask for much more. Yet there was still one more game to play.

The Sooners would be making a return engagement in the Orange Bowl on New Year's Day, and this time they'd be meeting unbeaten Florida State, which wanted a victory very badly so it could lay claim to the national championship. And in the first quarter it looked as if it might happen as the Seminoles marched in for the game's first score near the end of the initial period. The extra point made it a 7–0 game.

But then the Sooners settled down, and with Billy and quarterback J.C. Watts leading the way, they scored 17 points in the second period to take a 17–7 lead at halftime. In the second half the wishbone offense continued to roll up the yardage as the Sooner defense completely shut down the Seminole attack.

With about nine minutes left in the game, the Sooners began a 99-yard drive that would last 14 plays and eat up 7:13 on the clock. Finally with the ball at the Seminole 34, quarterback Watts kept the ball and rolled around end. He was hit after gaining 12 yards, but before he went down he pitched back to Billy who rambled 22 yards for the final score of the game and the final touchdown of his great Sooner career. Oklahoma won the game, 24–7, finished as the third ranked team in the country with an 11–1 mark, and Billy Sims wound up his career with 164 yards rushing. It was a fitting climax to two great seasons.

By then, of course, the speculation had already started. It wasn't so much where Billy would play as a pro, but how much money his immense talent would command and how he would fare as an NFL rookie in 1980. There have been plenty of college hotshots who have fizzled quickly in the pros for a variety of reasons. One man who thought Billy was a sure bet was Tommy Prothro, the Director of Player Personnel for the Cleveland Browns and a former college and NFL head coach.

"There are six or seven good backs coming out of the colleges this year," said Prothro, "and one great one. The great one is Billy Sims and the way I see it he's close to being an Earl Campbell or Walter Payton. He weighs about 215 pounds and is as elusive as a 175-pounder. He's also got great moves and he doesn't have to stop to put a move on; he's always going up the field. He has great strength in his legs, runs through and over tacklers, and he's going to be great at catching the ball."

Some agreed with Prothro, a few disagreed, claiming Billy might not be fast enough to be a real breakaway threat and not big enough to be a power runner. But most football people acknowledged that he should be a fine addition to any team. Because of NFL draft rules, there was no doubt which team would have the first shot at him. It would be the club with the poorest record in 1979.

That was the Detroit Lions, a team that had finished with a humiliating 2–14 mark in '79, earning the dubious distinction of the number one pick. There was little doubt it would be Billy, though the Lions still had the option of trading the number one draft right to another team for several players. That's how the Dallas Cowboys drafted Tony Dorsett and the Houston Oilers Earl Campbell. Both teams gave up several good players to get a great one. Sometimes teams with 2–14 records can make better use of three or four good players to fill holes rather than one potentially great star.

But this did not seem to be the case in Detroit. For one thing, the Lions were not an expansion team trying to build up a stable personnel. They were a proud old franchise that had started play in the NFL way back in 1934. A year later they won their first championship. They did it again in 1952 and '53, beating the Cleveland Browns in the title game both times.

The following year they were there again, losing to the Browns for the crown. But they came back to win another one in 1957, making them one of the dominant teams of the 1950s. The team was up and down in the '60s, finishing second in its division a number of times, but never breaking through, and the pattern repeated in the '70s, though the club was more around the .500 mark. Yet the Lions always played good competitive football.

They were in the so-called "Black and Blue" division, the NFC Central, with long-time rivals Chicago, Minnesota, and Green Bay, and from 1977, the Tampa Bay Buccaneers. The division was known for its rock 'em, sock 'em football, with a lot of hitting. From 1976 through 1978, the Lions compiled records of 6–8, 6–8, and 7–9. They were obviously not a top team during this period, but often seemed on the brink of breaking through, especially after the appointment of Monte Clark as head coach in January of 1978.

Then came 1979 and disaster. But in the minds of many, the Lions were not a 2–14 team. For one thing, they had lost their quarterback, Gary Danielson, who was just coming into his own. He went down with a knee injury in the final preseason game and didn't play once all year, and the team relied on an untried youngster. There were also other injuries and bad breaks, and Coach Clark was optimistic about the team's immediate future.

"First of all, we won't make the mistake of allowing last year's results affect this year's thinking," he said. "We're just going to forget what happened in '79, the sooner the better. There was no great mystery as to what went wrong. It's pretty tough operating without your top quarterback and a few other key people.

"So I just don't believe we have 2–14 personnel. Even with all the problems last season we weren't that far off. We were ahead in ten games and just couldn't hold the lead. And we lost eight games by eight points or less. So with the return of the injured players and the youngsters who gained experience, we could surprise some people. I fully expect a strong draft and the opportunity for some of the first year people to step in and really contribute."

With this kind of optimism, the first order of business was the draft. Unfortunately, there were some rumors going around before the Lions made a pick. Billy's agent in contract negotiations was a former dentist-turned-agent named Jerry Argovitz. Knowing the Lions had first choice of his client, he was said to have asked for a six-year package worth some $4.5 million, including a $1.5 million signing bonus, a $1 million loan, and another $2 million in salary. The story said the Lions had countered with an offer of $300,000 signing bonus and $100,000 loan. Soon it was apparent that preliminary negotiations were in progress and Argovitz was making it public.

"We're so far apart that we're not even in a bargaining position," he told the press. "There are running backs on the Houston Oilers who don't even play and make more than $100,000. What we're looking for is lifetime security, to sign a one-time contract with a team."

That would be a tall order for any team to fill, especially with the often short career-span of an NFL running back, where the injury risk runs very high. Suppose Billy or someone like him signed a long-time, big-bucks, no-cut, fully-guaranteed contract. Then in his first game comes a crippling knee injury. That leaves the team holding the bag. So it would be very difficult for any team to accept that kind of proposition.

As the draft came closer, Argovitz continued to apply the pressure and it became clear that feelings between him and the club were becoming bitter.

"Detroit has a once-in-a-lifetime chance to draft a player of Sims' magnitude and they're offering him below an average salary, less than some linebackers make," Argovitz said. "If the Lions don't sign him before the draft, they never will. He'll either play in Canada or sit out a year."

So Argovitz was making threats. There was little doubt that a Canadian team would love a player like Billy, but could they afford to pay him also? Who knows. But the agent wanted to keep the options open and he kept making noise.

"The Lions apparently don't want to pay Billy Sims and they don't want to trade him," he said. "It doesn't make sense. Billy would really like to play there. He likes the facilities and the players and was really impressed with Coach Monte Clark. And there's nobody else in the league anywhere who can do for Detroit what this young man can do. The fans want him, the team wants him, the coach wants him, and all he wants is a good paying job."

While Argovitz seemed to be the villain in this little scenario, he really wasn't. He was just doing his job, trying to get everything he could for his client. Various agents have different ways of doing their jobs. If there is a villain it's the system that has made so many dollars available to athletes.

Nevertheless, the gap between what was being asked and what was being offered was great. And by mid-April, with the draft still some two weeks away, the Lions were asking around, seeing what kind of package they could get for the rights to Billy. In fact, it was reported in the *Los Angeles Herald Examiner* that the Rams had turned down a deal for Billy because the Lions asking price was too steep, four or five good players. Yet the Detroit front office still claimed the team wanted Sims.

"We need a running back and he's the top guy," said Tim Rooney, whose job it was to evaluate available talent. "Any deal would have to knock our eyes out before we'd part with Sims. He means more to us than any combination of drafts and players. Nine or ten teams have inquired about him, but we haven't made a real effort to deal. We really like this guy."

With the draft just a day away, the situation was still not resolved, the two sides far apart. But no trade had been announced and it was assumed that the Lions would draft Billy as expected, then worry about signing him. Billy himself was headed to New York for the ceremonies, and the official NFL player profiles, featuring scouting reports on the prospective draftees, certainly made it sound as if Billy was the top choice.

"Complete package," the report read. "Speedy, innate runner with superior cutting ability . . . consistently made the first defender miss . . . explodes through holes/bounces off tacklers . . . great balance/body control . . . super acceleration/leg spring . . . fearless blocker . . . pass-receiving possibilities were not explored at Oklahoma."

Up to now, Billy had kept a very low profile, allowing Argovitz to do the negotiating. He just wanted to play football, but he was smart enough to know the realities of today's economy.

"I don't value money that much," he said. "Without a smart business manager I'd probably sign for $40,000 and be happy with it, because that would be more money than I've ever had. I do know there's no way I want to go to Canada to play. I'm ready to go to work for the Detroit Lions.

They just need an added touch, and I believe I'm that added touch."

Finally, the drama ended. The Detroit Lions made Billy Sims the number one draft choice of the entire National Football League. Now, they just had to sign him, and after the draft Billy finally started getting into the act.

"Everybody is making a 100 percent effort except Lions general manager Russ Thomas," he said. "It's up to him to wake up. But I'm optimistic that things will work out because I have an outstanding business manager."

Billy was in New York for the draft, as is the custom with the league's top choice. He tasted some of the glamour and excitement accorded the number one pick by appearing on several local and national TV shows, and getting the VIP treatment everywhere. The only thing that dampened it all was the persistent questions about his signing and the huge amount of money his agent was asking for, but Billy handled himself well.

"I'm excited about playing in the NFL," he said. "I know it's going to be hard work, but I'm used to that. Hopefully I can continue to do the things I did in college, carry them right over into pro ball. I think I can do it with the right caliber people and a team working together for a common goal. If everyone stays healthy and enjoys what they're doing, we should do well, and hopefully I can bring in some different type of attitude toward winning."

Billy then showed that he really wanted to play for the Lions by attending their three-day rookie camp in early May. In most cases, unsigned players avoid this kind of thing. Any kind of freak injury could quickly dissipate their negotiating positions.

But Billy wanted the coaches and his new team-mates to know he planned to be part of them. He also felt his attending was important for building the winning attitude he spoke about. It was a worthwhile endeavor for both Billy and the others.

"I'm extremely fond of Coach Clark," Billy said, after spending some time with the Lions' head man. "I can see in his personality that he really cares about his players. Sometimes that kind of caring is just as important as coaching. I can see he's no phony."

Clark, for his part, was also impressed. "Billy is really a class individual," the coach said. "He sent me a message before he arrived that said, 'Thank you for making me your number one selection. There will be no more two and fourteen seasons in Detroit.' That's the kind of attitude we need around here. I'm sure things will work out with the negotiations. I'm assuming that Billy will be in my backfield when training camp opens in July. He's what this team needs and he's what this town (Detroit) needs."

The coach said that Billy's speed, quickness, acceleration, receiving ability and strength compared favorably with the other great runners in the league, adding: "We're going to look for any way known to man to get the ball to him."

Billy, too, enjoyed the experience, saying that he had a great time and felt he could really contribute to the team. He then showed the kind of fiber he was made of by returning to Oklahoma to take his final exams so he could graduate with a bachelor's degree in recreational therapy. Billy liked to finish what he started.

That left it to Jerry Argovitz to fire the parting shot. He said that attending rookie camp was the final concession Billy would make and that he did it for Coach Clark. He added that their position had not basically changed. So in that sense, the stalemate continued.

By mid-May there were more rumors about Billy possibly playing in Canada. But the Saskatchewan team, which had the rights to Billy, just didn't have the money to make an offer. Negotiations with the Lions continued, and finally, the second week of June, it was resolved.

Billy signed a contract said to be the most lucrative ever given an NFL rookie. The terms of the contract were not disclosed, but hardliner Argovitz said he would not exchange it for the contract of any other player in the country. It was estimated by those close to the situation that the three-year package was around the $2 million mark, with a large signing bonus and good salary. At long last, Billy could concentrate on football.

"I'm glad it's all over with," he said. "I don't play negotiations, I play football. Now I have to go out and prove myself. The team needs a sparkplug and some motivation. You need that and a feeling of pulling together to win. It's a job, but it should be fun. And I believe in miracles."

Obviously, Billy was sky-high over signing and anxious to start playing again. But the events of the next few days would have him on steep roller coaster. A day or so after signing, he got some more good news. He had been named Big Eight Conference Athlete of the Year for 1979-80. But just when everything seemed to be falling into place, tragedy struck.

Billy learned that his seventeen-year-old brother, Dale, whose handicap had spurred Billy to study and work with retarded youngsters, had drowned in a swimming pool accident. It was a shattering blow and Billy's first reaction was said to be, "I'd rather it had been me than him." The two were always very close.

Jerry Argovitz, Billy's agent, said that immediate plans were being made to start a foundation in Billy's name to raise money for handicapped youngsters. It would be called the Billy Sims Mental Retardation Foundation. The entire tragic incident served to show the depth of Billy's character. He had been working with retarded youngsters before, but the shock of his brother's death only made him increase his efforts on behalf of others.

Finally, by the end of July it was time for camp to begin. Billy drove to Michigan from Oklahoma, towing a trailer with his furniture. In spite of his huge contract, he was a man of simple tastes, without the fancy frills. No gold chains, jewelry, luxury car. By contrast, he drove a Chevy Blazer, and did most of the mechanical work on it himself. It was obvious that Billy Sims from Hooks, Texas, wasn't about to change.

"I'm tight with the bucks," he admitted. "I've always felt it isn't how much you make, but how much you keep. And since I'm basically the same cheap person I've always been, I intend to keep a lot of it."

Once in camp, Billy thought only of football. He was confident in his ability, but expressed some worry about the long NFL schedule, with four preseason and sixteen regular-season games.

"It's almost the equivalent of two college seasons," he said, "and I'm a bit concerned about how to handle it. Sounds like it's almost a matter of survival. I don't see how I can carry the ball thirty or thirty-five times every game like I did at Oklahoma. That's a lot of pounding for twenty games."

Of course, Billy didn't carry quite that much at Oklahoma, and Coach Clark wasn't about to overwork his prize rookie and chance burning him out. Besides, with quarterback Danielson fully recovered from his knee injury, the team had one of the finest young passers in the game. They also had another fine running back in Dexter Bussey. So the burden wouldn't be Billy's alone.

If Billy was concerned about the pounding, he didn't show it. As camp opened, he never gave less than 100 percent. And when he broke the ice with his remark about being the reason none of the veterans got raises, he was quickly accepted as a regular guy. No prima donna was this Billy Sims. And no slouch with the football. The second time he touched the ball in the first scrimmage of the year, he burst through a hole in the right side of the line and sprinted 65 yards for a touchdown.

"I looked over at Coach Clark and he had goose pimples," said quarterback Danielson, speaking of Billy's run. It was as if they all knew they had something, the explosive offensive player the team had lacked for so long.

After the first week of camp, Billy had impressed his teammates not only as a player, but as a person as well.

"He's a super person to get along with," said veteran linebacker Charlie Weaver. "I don't think he'll be making any enemies here. Being a young player you'd expect him to come in with a Rolls Royce and flashing the big money. But he's not doing any of that. He's just one of the guys."

Defensive tackle John Woodcock added, "You see a guy getting all that money and you begin to wonder about him. But when you meet a guy like

Billy, it makes you feel really good for him."

As for Coach Clark, he couldn't say enough about the youngster from Hooks. "Billy has great work habits," the coach said, "and he has great pride. He's very alert and always aware of what's going on. And he doesn't hold back with anything. On blocking drills he sticks his head right in there."

"He hasn't really surprised me," said quarterback Danielson. "I expected a lot from him and that's what he's shown. He's just very determined to be a good football player. I met him over the winter and had the feeling then that he didn't want to come in as a hot dog, and the more I'm around him the more convinced I am that I was right. More than anything else, Billy wants to be a force in the National Football League."

Being accepted by his new teammates was very important to Billy. "I just came in here to be myself," he said. "Regardless of what I've done in the past I want to be treated like everyone else. There will be people who take things the wrong way. They figure you owe them something and expect you to be available constantly. For instance, there are times when people are asking for autographs when I have to say 'not now.' I have to have some time to myself. But if I don't sign autographs in the morning, I make sure to sign them in the afternoon."

As training camp dissolved into the preseason games, it became quickly evident that Billy was living up to advance notices. He was playing extremely well and becoming an integral part of the team. There would be no need to ease him into the lineup gradually, as is the case with some talented rookies who require extra time to learn a new system. Billy was the acknowledged starting halfback almost from day one. In fact, the starting halfback from the previous season and the team's best runner before Billy, Dexter Bussey, volunteered to move to fullback. He knew that was the only way he'd get to play.

By the time the Lions buried the New Orleans Saints in their third preseason game, Billy Sims was already a force to be reckoned with, and the team was looking anything like a 2–14 football club. In fact, to some they looked like playoff contenders. Quarterback Danielson was back and playing very well. Yet whenever he had the chance, he would sing the praises of his new halfback.

"A runner like Billy makes a big difference," the quarterback said. "He's a new ingredient; he gives us a new dimension, even when he doesn't have the ball. For example, the first two passes I threw tonight began as fakes to Billy. The fakes held the linebackers in because they feared Billy's running. That gave me more throwing time and more throwing area.

"I'm still not quite used to him and he fools me sometimes. I get the feeling he's running at three-quarter speed, but he's really just being patient. When he sees an opening, he has a great burst of speed. He can read blocks extremely well and cut off them very quickly."

Though Billy didn't have any real long runs against the Saints, he had several dazzling bursts, including a brilliant, 11-yard touchdown jaunt in which he left tacklers sprawled over the field. The way he cut and juked, and slid through holes impressed even the usually cynical Detroit writers, many of whom were already calling him the best running back the Lions had ever had. But Billy himself wasn't quite satisfied. He felt there were still adjustments to be made.

"I still have a long way to go," he said. "I know I'm not going to have the same kind of long runs I had at Oklahoma. The pro game is different. And I'm still learning. There was a dropped pass tonight that shouldn't have happened. The team is still working on more pass plays for me, though I'd still rather just run the ball because the more I run, the better I get. But a pro back has to catch the ball and I'm aware of that. So there's still a lot of work to be done."

With the regular season fast approaching, Billy knew it was time for the end of the talk and beginning of action. But many of his enthusiastic teammates couldn't help talking about his various attributes whenever they were asked.

"Billy has incredible quickness and that's important," said assistant coach Don Doll. "But the two things that really make him stand out are his aptitude for the game and his competitiveness. He instinctively makes the right move at the right time and he's a burning competitor who will challenge anybody."

Defensive Coordinator Maxie Baughan, a former all-pro linebacker, talked about Billy's mental toughness.

"All the really great runners have it," he said. "And that kind of mental toughness makes them difficult to intimidate. As a defensive coach, I see football as basically a game of intimidation. If you can hit them hard enough to discourage them, you've got a good chance of winning. If you can't intimidate them with hard hits, then the defense becomes discouraged. The back that I played against who was the most difficult to intimidate was Gale Sayers, and Billy Sims reminds me a lot of him."

Fast company. But Billy would have to prove it in the opener against one of the most intimidating defenses in the entire NFL, that of the Los Angeles Rams. And the team would be playing away, at the Rams new home in Anaheim, which would make their first test doubly difficult.

The Lions kicked off and seconds later they were trailing, 6–0. L.A.'s Drew Hill took the kickoff on his own two and lugged it back 98 yards for a score. What a way to start the season, great for the Rams, awful for the Lions. The extra point was missed, but the main damage was done. Billy hadn't been on the field yet and his club was already trailing, while the fans watching on TV back in Detroit must have been crooning about the same old Lions.

Then Detroit got the ball and quarterback Danielson decided to let Billy get loose. He gave him the ball four straight times. He gained two, then 11, then three, then lost one. But it helped him leave the pre-game jitters behind and get right into the flow. The team drove downfield to the Rams 35, then stalled. But rookie placekicker Ed Murray came on and shocked everyone with a mammoth, 52-yard field goal, putting the Lions right back in it at 6–3.

The next time they got the ball at their own nine, and immediately embarked on a long, 91-yard drive. And unlike Lion teams of the past several years, they were chewing it up on the ground. Both Billy and Dexter Bussey were ripping off sizable gains against the vaunted Rams defense. Billy looked strong and confident, hitting the holes quickly and proving very hard to take down.

With the ball on the Detroit ten he got it again. This time there was no stopping him as he roared into the end zone with the first touchdown of his NFL career. Murray's kick made it a 10–7 game at the end of one. But then the Rams came back, and rolled to two quick scores at the outset of the second period, jumping back on top by a 20–10 count. Could the rout be on now?

With time running out in the first half, the Lions drove downfield again. Finally, with the ball on the one and just 24 seconds left, Danielson gave it to Billy. He burst into the end zone, holding the ball in his left hand away from his body and lowering his right hand to about an inch from the ground in an effort to keep his balance, which he did. Even the partisan L.A. crowd roared its approval. The kick made it a 20–17 game at the half.

In the second half the Lions took charge, their offense exploding and their defense shutting down the Rams. First they drove down so Murray could kick a 38-yard field goal to tie the game. Then they got the ball back and started again. The key play was what started out as a short Danielson pass to Billy. When linebacker Bob Brudzinski stumbled slightly, Billy blew right by him. Then he sprinted past rookie defensive back Johnnie Johnson, a blue chipper, and lugged the ball sixty yards downfield before he was angled out of bounds. Two plays later Bussey took it in from the 15, giving the Lions the lead for the last time.

The fourth period saw them get two more. The first one was vintage Sims, shades of Oklahoma, as he put on a show with a dazzling, 41-yard TD burst, his third score of the game. The final score made it a 41-20 Lions victory. It was hard to believe.

It was also hard to believe Billy's NFL debut. It was incredible. He spearheaded a Lion attack that rolled up 494 yards of total offense, with 330 coming on the ground. In his first pro effort, Billy carried the ball 22 times, getting 153 big yards. He also grabbed two passes for 64 yards. And with the defense keying on Billy, Dexter Bussey ran for 111 yards on 14 tries. It was the first time two Detroit backs had gone over 100 yards in the same game since 1934.

Quarterback Danielson also showed he had regained his touch with ten completions in nineteen attempts for 173 yards in his first regular-season game in nearly two years. It was obvious that the team had shored itself up all-around, but it was equally obvious that the biggest difference, the catalyst for the whole thing, was Billy Sims.

"Billy Sims does not require us to play any differently," said star offensive tackle Keith Dorney. "We block exactly the same way for him as for any other back. But he just hits the hole so quickly that he makes us look good. He's so quick that I don't get to see many of his runs. I have to tell by the roar of the crowd."

"If you think Billy is good now, wait till you see him in our eighth game," said Danielson. "I said in preseason that he was holding back. What I've said all fall is that he'll make everybody else better. For instance, the offensive line loves blocking for him because they know he'll pick up the big gains."

"Billy Sims was everything he's supposed to be," said Coach Clark, who added, "The whole team deserves a lot of credit. Especially after having the opening kickoff rammed down its throat. They certainly showed a maturity they didn't have in the past. What happened today was no accident and we couldn't be happier."

Billy, too, was extremely happy, and as usual, his

first thoughts were for the team.

"We're for real," he said. "I know we are capable of getting the job done, and I hope this game shows everyone that we're in this thing all the way. As for myself, I was expecting to do well and didn't feel any pressure whatsoever. I did study the game plan very intently and had good up front blocking. There were still a couple of plays when I went outside instead of inside where the play was supposed to be, but I broke 'em out, anyway. There's still plenty of work to be done, especially on my pass routes."

The Rams players were equally impressed with the Oklahoma thunderbolt who had hit them so suddenly and so hard.

"He's as good as any back in the league," said veteran linebacker Jack Reynolds. And another linebacker, Bob Brudzinski, added, "That man can do some running, spinning, turning, and breaking tackles."

The team really showed its mettle and new attitude the following week. They were meeting division and longtime rivals, the Green Bay Packers and the game had a special significance to all the Lions. Three days before the game, Gary Danielson's infant daughter had died, but the courageous quarterback decided to play.

"He's the heart and soul of our ballclub," Coach Clark said. "Gary's the leader, the glue that keeps us together."

The whole team didn't want to let Danielson down, and they played brilliantly once again. Once more it was Billy's running that set up the entire Lions' offense. Murray kicked a pair of field goals to give Detroit a 6-0 lead early in the second period. But the Packers came back to score and

take a 7–6 advantage. That didn't deter the Lions.
They were playing with confidence and embarked
on another long drive, Danielson's accurate passing offsetting Billy's nifty runs. Finally Billy lugged
it in from the one, giving the lead back to the
Lions. Another Murray field goal made it a16–7 at
the half.

In the final two periods it was all Detroit. Two
more field goals made it 22–7. Then in the final session Detroit had the ball at its own 13. Danielson
faded back and looked deep. With his receivers
covered he spotted Billy cutting across the middle
as a secondary receiver. He hit him and Billy went
into his act, faking several defenders and bursting
into the clear. He seemed to slow down near the
goal line, but when safety Johnnie Gray came up,
he calmly pushed him away with a stiff-arm and
went in to complete an 87-yard touchdown romp.
That also made the final score, 29–7.

For the second straight week Billy was outstanding. He carried the ball twenty times and gained 134
yards, plus he grabbed two more passes for 94
yards. Danielson also excelled with an 11–17 day,
good for 246 yards. And the defense again played
very well. After just two weeks Billy was leading
the entire NFL in rushing with 287 yards on 42
carries for an outstanding 6.8 per try average. He
expected to do even better.

"I believe those 200-yard days will come," he
said. "They always have, ever since I've been
playing. I didn't feel real loose out there today. It
was kind of cold. That's why I pulled up on the
long pass play. I felt a slight twinge in my upper leg
and I didn't want to risk pulling anything, so I relied on the straight-arm instead."

"We're going to watch Billy carefully," said

Danielson. "We're not going to burn him out by using him too much. You can't run your whole offense around one person. We've got a lot of offense here and we're gonna use it. The thing that's making me happiest about Billy, by the way, is his catching. When I saw him in camp I thought he was a natural receiver, and it's beginning to look as if I was right."

And offensive guard Russ Bolinger talked about the fierce competitor that Billy is during the game. "I looked at Billy in the huddle today," said Bolinger, "and it was like he was possessed. He just wanted the ball."

A week later the team was home in the Detroit Silverdome, and Billy would be trying to become the first rookie to gain over 100 yards in each of his first three games. The opponent was the St. Louis Cardinals, not known for a rugged defense.

It was a hard-fought game all the way. The Lions took a 10–7 lead at halftime, then scored 10 more in the final period for a 20–7 victory, their third straight. Billy had another good game, gaining 95 yards on 25 tough carries and scoring once on a thirteen-yard run. He also had a seven-yard TD run called back because of a penalty. Had that been allowed to stand, he would have had the record.

"In my heart I feel I've done it," he said, afterward. "But the most important thing is winning the game. I'm used to that, and the only record I'm interested in is the number of W's in those weekly standings."

By now, the Lions were the surprise team of the league and the following week they would host another long-time Central Division rival, the Minnesota Vikings. Would the bubble burst? Once again it was a close game for a half, being tied at 7–7. But Billy Sims was all over the field, picking up a lot of yardage. He seemed on his way to another big day, though the game was still up for grabs.

The Lions had been dominating second halves all year long and today they did it again. A Murray field goal made it 10–7 in the third, then in the final session they got two scores within 18 seconds. First Danielson culminated a drive with a five-yard TD toss to Freddie Scott. Then on the first play after the kickoff, defensive back Ray Oldham stole the ball from the Vikes' Ted Brown and ran 29 yards for a score. The final was 27–7 and the Lions were still unbeaten.

As for Billy, he was superb once again. He carried the ball 27 times and gained 157 yards. He also caught three passes for 26 more. After four weeks he had gained 539 yards on 94 carries for a 5.7 average and the NFL lead. He learned later that he had been named Offensive Player of the Month for September.

After the Minnesota game, Billy was given the game ball by his teammates. But he didn't keep it for long. Defensive end William Gay brought a young boy into the lockerroom. The boy was twelve years old and in a wheelchair. He was suffering from muscular dystrophy. He loved being in the lockerroom and loved meeting Billy Sims. Then, quietly, and without fanfare, Billy took his game ball and placed it gently on the youngster's lap. It was something the boy would cherish forever, and Billy Sims would get many more before he hung up his cleats.

With the team at 4–0, the city of Detroit had renewed its love affair with the Lions and started a new one with Billy Sims. In fact, local discos had a new dance called the Billy Sims Tilt and at one shopping mall, some 29,000 Billy Sims posters were sold in just two days. Billy also made appearances at local stores to sign autographs, and at one session there were an estimated 7,000 people waiting to see their newest hero. After the first two games a bumper sticker appeared that read, "From Worst (2–14) to First (2-0); Thank You, Mr. Sims." Billy was also getting endorsements and other fringe benefits befitting his fast start which had elevated him to instant superstar status.

But back on the football field the team and Billy both got a very rude awakening. The Atlanta Falcons put the clamps on the Detroit attack and on Billy Sims. Atlanta jumped off to a 17-3 lead after one period and increased it to 34–6 at the half. That was all she wrote, as they say. Playing catch-up, the Lions had to abandon the offense that worked for them through four games. Even when Billy did get the ball, he was stopped cold by a swarming, Atlanta defense, one that was obviously keying on him.

Danielson's passing rallied the team for 22 fourth period points, but they were still beaten for the first time, 43–28. And Billy, for the first time, saw the other side of playing running back in the NFL. He carried fourteen times and gained just 21 yards, less than two yards a pop, and he was battered by the Falcons all afternoon. Danielson, on the other hand, threw for 348 yards and three scores. Much of that came, however, when the game was already lost. The offense wasn't balanced. For his part, Billy had no excuses.

"Atlanta is just a good defensive team," he said. "They were well prepared and keying on me. Also, we ran fewer slants than we had been running.

We'll just have to make up for it next week."

The next game was against the lowly New Orleans Saints, a good game for a team trying to get back its rhythm. The Lions won it, 24–13, as Billy got 91 yards on 23 carries, grabbed four passes for another 62 yards, and scored twice. He was proving more and more effective as a pass receiver. The Lions were still leading their division at 5–1, and Billy continued to pace all NFL runners, with 651 yards, some seventy yards ahead of Chicago's great Walter Payton, and the two teams would be meeting head-on the following week.

Unfortunately, the game was similar in some ways to the Atlanta game. Chicago jumped on top, and the Lions had to play from behind, and when it's against a rock-ribbed defense, that isn't easy. The Bears took the lead with a touchdown in the first period, collected a field goal in the second, and another TD in the third. That made it 17–0, and an exchange of scores in the final session just upped it to 24–7.

Billy was limited to 14 carries and managed 53 yards. Payton gained 101 yards, but needed 27 totes to do it. So their rate of production was about the same. Neither had a great game. The main worry was that the Lions were not playing the kind of dominant football they had early in the season. Against the Bears they had one score called back by penalty, had a field goal try blocked, and fumbled the ball four times, losing one. And they were beginning to lose some key people to injuries.

Hoping to get back into the win column, the Lions traveled to Kansas City to face the rejuvenated Chiefs. And this one was a cliffhanger from the opening kickoff. It was scoreless in the first period. Then the Chiefs drew first blood with a long field goal. Minutes later they scored a touchdown to make it 10–0. But the Lions didn't panic. They calmly drove downfield and Murray booted a twenty-yard field goal before the half to keep it close at 10–3.

The Chiefs were also making it tough for Billy, holding him to just 29 yards in the first half. But after intermission, it was a different Billy Sims who was on the football field. It was if he just made up his mind . . . enough of this. It's been happening too often lately. He began chewing up the yards. Midway through the third period the ball was on the K.C. 45. Billy swept around right end, made a few quick cuts, and was off to the end zone with the tying score.

In the fourth period the Chiefs retook the lead, scoring to make it 17–10. But the Lions came back, Billy again leading a long drive and taking it in from the one. Murray's kick knotted it again at 17–17. It was a game that would go right down to the wire. Unfortunately, for the Lions, K.C. got the last laugh as Nick Lowery booted a 40-yard field goal with just 1:14 remaining to give the Chiefs a 20–17 victory.

The loss put a damper on Billy's outstanding performance. He had gained 126 yards in the second half to finish with 155 yards on 28 carries. But the Lions had suffered their third loss in four games and finished the first half of the season with a 5–3 record. They were still atop the division, but not playing well enough to be certain of a playoff berth.

As for Billy, he had completed the first half of his first pro season in fine style. His 859 yards on 173 carries were the best in the league. Houston's great Earl Campbell, playing in the AFC, was next with 807. Then came Payton at 762. Projected over the full season, Billy would finish around the 1,700 yard mark. But projecting and actually doing it were two different things, and the Lions did not look like the same confident steamroller that had won its first four games.

By the next week, those close to the team could see a slight difference in the attack. The passing game was suddenly taking precedence over the run. Part of the problem was injuries. The team had lost three of the five starters on the offensive line, including tackle Keith Dorney, who was having an outstanding year. That cost the club the delicate balance between blocker and runner, undoubtedly causing Billy and the other backs to lose some effectiveness.

The next game against the San Francisco 49ers was a good example. It was a sloppy game, poorly played. At one point the Lions turned the ball over five straight times. They finally got the go-ahead score with just 3:42 left. Then they held their breaths as 49er tight end Charles Young dropped an easy pass in the end zone that could have won it with just 46 seconds left. The final score was 17–13, but not a victory to be very proud about, not in the context of the early-season triumphs. As Coach Clark said,

"By the grace of God, he (Charles Young) didn't catch the ball. That was one we needed badly, but I feel for Bill Walsh."

As for Billy, he was more effective as a pass receiver than a runner for the first time. On the ground he gained just 37 yards in 17 rushes. Yet he caught 11 passes for 96 yards, including a 41-yard touchdown. And for the first time all season he wasn't the NFL's top runner. Earl Campbell had passed him.

Then the team hit a low point, a 34–0 shellacking by the Vikings. Seven fumbles and eight sacks contributed to the downfall and for the first time there were stories of team dissension. Billy had just 21 yards on nine carries and wasn't looking anything like the superstar rookie he had been most of the season.

Apparently there were problems between Coach Clark and general manager Russ Thomas, and quarterback Danielson was the one who spoke out, saying the GM was becoming too involved in coaching decisions. And there were still many veterans disgruntled with their contracts. One of them, defensive tackle John Woodcock, had actually quit the team after the eighth game. To their credit, most of the players didn't blame Billy for this. For his part, he kept a low profile through it all. Danielson was the chief spokesman for the unhappy players. And as the QB and team leader, it was his place to assume that role.

The team tried to rally the next week against Baltimore, but they still couldn't regain the spark. The Colts beat them, 10–9, despite 126 yards by Billy on 30 workhorse carries. That gave him 1,043 yards and made him the Lions' all-time season rushing leader, breaking the record of another Sooner, Steve Owens. But it didn't make Billy especially happy.

"I really don't care about being the greatest Lion or anything else," he said. "My main goal is to win games. We need to win and badly."

He was right. The club was at 6–5 and tied with the Vikings for the divisional lead. A playoff berth was now definitely in big doubt, especially the way they had been playing. Then against Tampa Bay they seemed to turn it around, winning 24–10, as Billy ground out 75 yards, hurt his shoulder in the third period, but returned in the fourth. This was the tough time of year and he was feeling the lumps. But the big win took some of the hurt away.

Then came the traditional Thanksgiving Day game, with the opponents the hated Bears. If anything, the game showed that the Lions lacked the ability to finish off an opponent. They had a 17–3 lead, but allowed the Bears to tie the game in regulation. The Bears received the kickoff in sudden-death overtime, and Dave Williams promptly lugged it back 95 yards to stun the Lions, 23–17. Billy had 72 yards, but Payton logged 123 in their head-to-head battle. The team was 7–6, tied with the Vikes, and there were three games left.

How was Billy bearing up under the pressure of the great start, then the dissension, then the close losses, and now the fight for a playoff berth. Finally speaking out, he seemed to have an inward calm, and a philosophy that would allow him to do his best, but not be torn apart by the happenings around him.

"Life goes on, man, no matter what," he said. "We're still a good team and it's not over yet. This kind of thing can really tear at you. In fact, I've seen football destroy a person. He gets too involved. I'm not that crazy about football. I'm not that gung-ho that I eat and sleep the game. I enjoy football, sure. But when it's over, I'm done with it. I go on to other things. It's not all there is in life."

Billy had to be philosophical. The next week the team lost a crucial game, 24–23, to the Cardinals. And they lost in again on a kick return, as St. Louis got a 57-yard punt return with just 3:40 left for the winning score. Billy had just 43 yards on 20 carries and suddenly everything seemed to be slipping away. Payton had even passed him in the NFC rushing race. The club was not 7–7 and a game behind Minnesota in the NFC Central. They had to finish first. Their record wasn't good enough to make the playoffs as a wild card.

To their credit, the team responded, winning its final two games, 27–14 over Tampa Bay, and 24–3 against Green Bay, giving them a 9–7 record for the year, quite a difference from the 2–14 of a year earlier. But Billy had a rugged finish. Against the Bucs he had his poorest rushing day of the season, 16 yards on 12 carries, and he capped it off with 54 on 18 against Green Bay.

Unfortunately for the Lions, the 9–7 mark wasn't good enough. The Vikings also finished at 9–7, but won the division because of a better record within the division.

"A 9–7 record is not where we wanted to be," said Coach Clark. "But it represents a heck of a lot of progress from last season. And we've got a lot of good prospects staring us in the face. Everybody is excited about next year."

The coach also praised the season of his first-year running back, Billy Sims. "Look at his production. A lot of great backs haven't done the things he's done in his first year, ever."

It was true. Billy gained more yards as a rookie than anyone except Earl Campbell and Otis Anderson. He finished the year with 1,303 yards on 313 carries for a 4.2 average and NFL leading 16 touchdowns. Because of his dropoff in the final games, he was fourth in NFC rushing behind Payton, Anderson, and William Andrews of Atlanta. But even more of a surprise were his 51 pass receptions, second on the team. It got him another 621 yards and a 12.2 average per catch. That's a very high average for a running back. Three of his 16 TD's came via the pass. Not bad for a guy who caught just three passes in his high school and college careers.

In addition, he set a slew of team records, was everybody's Rookie of the Year, and made a number of all-pro teams as a freshman. His season could have been even greater had not both Billy and the team slowed the last half of the year. He gained 859 yards the first eight games, and just 444 in the final eight. And in his last three games he had just 113 yards on 50 tries for a 2.2 average. It could be that the long NFL season got to him.

"I often felt I had to get the ball to him or fake it to him on almost every play," said Gary Danielson after the season. "Billy carried a lot early in the year and I'm sure there was a lot of wear and tear on him."

That has to be true. He carried the ball in pre-season, then got it 313 times during the regular campaign. The most he carried at Oklahoma was 231 times and while catching but two passes. With the Lions, he grabbed 51 passes, and that means getting hit a lot more. He also had to block more with the Lions, for both the run and the pass. In addition, both Billy and the team's fast start may have spoiled some people. The Lions just weren't as good as they seemed in the early going, especially when injuries took out some key people in the trenches. There were other breakdowns the last half of the year.

Yet it was still a remarkable year, witnessed by the fact that only two rookie runners had ever done

better. And with his bitter and public salary negotiations and subsequent large contract, Billy had to
win over a lot of people.

Listen to what veteran defensive back Jimmy Al-
len had to say. "Billy's not lazy. You see him in the
weight room, working. You see him on the practice
field, working. The veterans, well, we hear so much
about a new guy, we want to check him out. Billy
checks."

And to former Lions star runner, Mel Farr, still
a Detroit resident: "This city was starved for something. It was a loser. Now it has fallen in love with
Billy Sims. He's the right person for the right time,
the hottest commodity to hit this town in a long
time."

Yet in a sense, there are two Billy Sims, and it
seems to be a healthy situation, where one gives
strength to the other. How else could he cope so
well with both success and adversity? His immediate goal is to be as good a football player as he can
be. But he has a long range goal, also. Coach
Monte Clark told a story that perhaps describes
Billy Sims the football player.

"We were playing St. Louis and had a fourth
and one. Big play. Billy got the ball and went for it.
He was really stung by a linebacker at the line of
scrimmage. You could hear the crack of the
helmets on the sideline. But he rolled off to get the
first down by inches.

"That's why he's such a great player. He rises to
the occasion. He has that same thing Jim Brown
had, that vibration. You can see it in him and you
just get him the ball."

And the other Billy Sims, in his own words.
"When it ends, when the money stops coming in,

I'll never look back. I'll be back in Hooks, and I'll be happy. In fact, I'll only be happy in Hooks. I'll say I enjoyed football and I was good at it. But now let someone else do it. I'm just a country boy, and in a way I was tired of all this even when I was in college. I can't wait for when the time comes for me to say, well, it's over. I'm goin' home."

That's quite an admission from quite a football player, and one who is undoubtedly going to get better. But to those who have always known him, or have met him along the way, the sentiment seems most unanimous. Billy Sims from Hooks, Texas, is also quite a man.

Russ Francis

To many people within the football community, Russ Francis is an enigma. In one sense, he completely fits the mold, possessing the perfect blend of skills and talents for his position. Yet at the same time he throws the mold away. His lifestyle is often puzzling, distracting, and sometimes even annoying to people who feel that football superstars must have a certain kind of attitude at all times.

Since coming into the National Football League in 1975, the all-pro tight end of the New England Patriots has become the prototype or model for the position. At 6′-6″, 240-pounds, Russ has the size and strength of an interior lineman. So he can go head to head with a defensive end or linebacker. Yet at the same time he's got deep speed, the kind of speed that can outrun defensive backs. And he can catch the ball in traffic and leg it like a fullback if the occasion calls for it.

There might be some tight ends a bit faster, and maybe a few who can block a bit better. A couple might be better leapers for a tough catch. But it is the combination of all the skills that makes Russ Francis close to being the perfect tight end for today's game. The only other player who perhaps does all these things as well as Russ is Dave Casper, now with the Houston Oilers, after spending the first part of his career with the Oakland Raiders.

Knowing these facts, people probably often picture Russ as one of those kids who ate, drank, and slept football for years, had a brilliant college career, and came into pro football determined to give every ounce of his strength and his time to the game. Well, they should guess again and get ready to meet the other side of Russ Francis.

For openers, he grew up in Hawaii and lives there in the off-season today. He loves the sun and the surf. He rides a motorcycle. He flies his own plane. He has spent time as a professional wrestler. And his most recent passion is skydiving. In other words, show Russ Francis something new, different, and exciting, and he'll want to try it. As he himself has said:

"I've always believed there is much more in life than football, and I want to sample and know as much as I can."

Now don't get the wrong idea. Russ Francis is serious about football. Like most other stars, he wants to be the best player he can be. But he does things his own way, and in the world of the NFL, that isn't always understood. Nor is his lifestyle. Most people just can't comprehend how a high-priced superstar could gamble on losing it all by something as risky as sky-diving. But Russ has already come close, surviving a bad motorcycle accident, yet he doesn't seem ready to change.

He's even come under criticism from teammates who don't think he's always putting out. But again, it's hard for most players to fathom this very individualistic and different kind of man. But for everything Russ Francis is, there is one thing he isn't. He isn't reluctant to talk about the situation.

"I get a lot of letters from people asking why I do some of the things I do," Russ says. "People will even write and ask why I take my helmet off after a play as if I'm showing off. These people are half a mile away, so what can they see? The reason I take my helmet off is simple. It's uncomfortable."

Russ continues: "Sometimes when I speak to the press and don't want to talk about just football, they get angry. So what it amounts to is that I often get a lot of hostility just for being myself.

"I guess there are times when it looks as if I'm not really trying, or that I'm cocky. I've gotten that kind of feedback from some of my coaches. Even in college the coach came up to me once and said I was catching the ball so easily that I must be doing something wrong. I told him I could always catch the ball easily, but he still wanted me to change. Then when I came to the pros, one of our coaches told me I would have to try harder if I wanted to make it in this league. I was trying hard, but with my style in my own way."

Perhaps when you are a big, strong, handsome, and talented as Russ Francis, people just expect more. And it hasn't helped the situation that Russ's team, the New England Patriots, has a league-wide reputation for not living up to its potential. For about five years now, the Patriots have had outstanding personnel, the best in the league according to some. Therefore, at the outset of each season, there are so-called experts picking the team to reach or even win the Super Bowl. Yet each time the team has been knocked off early in the playoffs or failed to make it there at all.

To make matters worse, there have been a number of internal problems, including holdouts by star players and a strange resignation by a head coach. So put all these problems together with a highly individualistic player like Russ, and his problems shouldn't come as a surprise.

Yet through it all, Russ continues to hold the reputation as one of the very best in the business. He has fought his way through a number of serious injuries and has played hurt on more than more occasion. Say what you want about his lifestyle and personality, but no one has ever questioned his guts.

Russ Francis was born on April 3, 1953, in Seattle, Washington, the third of six children born to Ed and Arlene Francis. At the time Russ was born, Ed Francis was a professional wrestler and his wife stayed at home. Later, when all the children were born, Mrs. Francis became a registered nurse.

While Russ was just an infant, Ed Francis was out on the wrestling circuit. He made enough money to support the family, but saved very little on top of that. Finally, when Russ was six, Gentleman Ed, as he was known in wrestling circles, decided the family needed a change of scenery. He announced that they would be moving to Hawaii.

"Dad borrowed some money, gave away our car, and the next thing I knew we were walking on Waikiki Beach," is the way Russ remembers it. "Dad was still low on money, so he suggested we sleep right on the beach for a few nights. That's what we did, slept right under a big tree. In fact, the tree is still there and I go back to visit it once in a while as a kind of memorial."

Ed Francis was a good father. He was a rough, physical man in some ways. His very profession dictated that. But he was also gentle and affectionate. In fact, both parents were very caring. Arlene Francis had some background in psychology and that helped her teach her children good manners, how to share things, and how to show respect.

Russ was also learning the joys of the outdoors life. As a youngster in Hawaii there was plenty of sand, sunshine, and the Pacific Ocean. It must have seemed like one, long summer vacation at a time. Russ and his friends spent hours combing the beaches and would often hunt for lizards, some of which they'd keep as pets. He couldn't think of a better place to live.

By the time Russ was ready for grade school, the family lived in Kailua, which is on the island of Oahu. He began playing sports then, too, although in Hawaii, there are always distractions. He wasn't like some of the kids in America, where the small-town kids are on the sandlots and the city kids on the playgrounds from dawn to dusk. Russ played, but it wasn't a passion.

He went out for Little League when he was old enough. Because there wasn't much baseball played in Hawaii, there weren't that many knowledgeable people, and he remembers that many of the teams didn't have good coaches so the kids didn't learn the finer points of the game. Fortunately, Russ had a good coach, a Japanese man who had learned the game in that baseball-crazed country. His last name was Fukunaga, but the boys called him Sunshine.

"I remember coming to practice with a new glove one day," Russ recalls. "Being a kid, I was really proud of that glove and didn't want to get it dirty. So when Sunshine began hitting me grounders I wouldn't put the glove all the way down and the ball kept going under it. He usually had a smile on his face, but this time he got mad. 'Get that glove dirty!' he shouted. Finally he just took the glove off my hand, dropped it on the ground, and stomped on it. It was dirty, all right, and after that I didn't miss any more ground balls."

His first taste of football came when he was in the sixth grade. Russ went out for a team in the Pop Warner League, and recalls that they "made me play with older kids because I was relatively big for my age."

Football really didn't kindle any fires within back then. Baseball was by far his favorite sport. He was a pitcher, and he recalls a time it gave him a real scare.

"For some reason, I always liked to throw things," he says. "I guess that's why I pitched in baseball, began as a quarterback in football, and later threw the javelin. Anyway, baseball was my big favorite while I was growing up. I was a pitcher, as I said, but one day I almost killed a guy and that really got to me.

"We were playing a semi-pro game and their bench was giving me a hard time. I got mad and decided to brush one of their hitters back just to quiet them down. Naturally, the pitch got away from me and hit the guy on the head. It cracked his batting helmet and put him in the hospital with a concussion."

Another testimony to Russ's throwing ability comes from a boyhood friend, Ken Anderson, who played ball with Russ right through high school.

"Yeah, Russ could throw as hard as anyone then," Anderson recalls. "As a kid I saw him actually break two catchers' mitts. And the guys on other teams were often afraid to get in the batter's box against him."

By the time he reached Kailua High School, Russ had experienced something that would always remain distasteful to him—racism. He became one of the victims. Because as a white person, he was in the minority among the natives of Hawaii. There was a word the natives used for a white person. . .haole. . .which was akin to many of the racial epithets used to describe various minorities in the United States. To be called a "haole" was an insult, often fighting words.

"I remember the last day of school being Kill-A-Haole-Day several years back then," Russ recalls. "And because of that there were a lot of fights. You didn't have much choice, either. You had to fight."

Of course, there were too many guys who went one-on-one with Russ, who was already big and strong, and quite an athlete. But he got in a few and the idea of the whole thing has made him extremely intolerant to any form of racism.

Russ went out for football at Kailua High and divided his time between quarterback and tight end, starting as a QB, switching to tight end, then coming back to quarterback as a senior. Though he was already a fine player, he still wasn't totally in love with the game and admitted that "I harbored some doubt about continuing as a player."

Maybe it was because there were so many distractions in Hawaii. Whatever there was to do, Russ did. He was already a surfer and a scuba diver, liked to sail, tried some high diving from the many cliffs on the islands, was climbing mountains and hang gliding. So he was already taking chances, putting his body and sometimes more on the line.

He learned to surf among breakers that sometimes were twenty feet high. Once on the north coast, he was dumped off his board as a giant wave broke over him. He couldn't hold the board and was dragged under. For a split second he thought he was going to die.

"A very calm feeling came over me," Russ recalls. "I remember thinking, 'This is it.' But I was calm and at the same time felt very sorry for my parents."

Fortunately, he came up and made it into shore. But even a close call like that didn't keep him from going back out and fighting the waves again. Give him a challenge and Russ responds.

By his senior year at Kailua, Russ was a fine player. He had been a tight end as a junior, but then they decided to put him back at quarterback. His friend, Ken Anderson, remembers:

"I remember being surprised that they switched him back because he was just becoming an outstanding tight end," Anderson says. "But I guess it was because of that great arm he had. Anyway, I was a receiver, too, and he always wanted to go out and practice together. His idea of that was to have me run as far downfield as I could and he'd throw it to me. And as far as I'd go, he'd still wing it over my head."

Russ had a good, but not great year on the gridiron. There was just too much position switching for him to really establish himself. And he was obviously too big to be a quarterback. But once the season ended, he decided to try something new. Once again it involved that strong right arm of his.

He began throwing the javelin, and he took to it like a fish takes to water.

There have been some other famous football players who threw the javelin. Perhaps the best known is Terry Bradshaw, the great quarterback of the Pittsburgh Steelers. When Bradshaw was a senior in high school back in 1966, he set a then national prep school all-time record by throwing the spear 244 feet, 11 inches. And Terry is reputed to have one of the strongest arms among all NFL signal-callers.

In the spring of 1971, Russ Francis was throwing for Kailua. Though still a relative newcomer to the sport, the big guy hurled the spear an incredible 259 feet, nine inches, and established a national high school mark that still stood as of 1980. The mammoth toss not only established Russ as the top high school thrower of all-time, but marked him as one of the best in the entire country. And there was talk that he had a shot at making the 1972 United States Olympic Team.

But events were happening very fast now in Russ's life and it was hard to say just where the next step would be taken. For one thing, Russ was certain he wanted to attend college. He was always a good student and at this point was beginning to harbor some thoughts about becoming a veterinarian. He loved animals and had a very strong belief in the importance of conservation.

"When somebody shows me his gun collection of some trophy mounted on the wall, it just makes me sick," he has said. "Morally, ·murder is murder."

So college was one consideration. He had also attended a summer football camp with his older brother, Billy, and was beginning to think he might like to continue in the sport after all. Yet his high school career was so uneven that there were not a slew of scouts coming after him, especially playing in Hawaii.

At the same time all this was happening, his family made another move. His father had been saving the money he made from wrestling and promotion, and decided to move everyone back to Oregon, where he bought a ranch. And knowing Russ, once he was on a ranch he had to try the cowboy life, and the challenge was at the rodeo, of course.

He tried his hand at that when he was just 18, and he still recalls vividly the first time he rode a bull. There was an old cowboy there who decided to help the big youngster rig his bull rope. Russ remembers him pulling it tighter and tighter, and finally wrapping it once around Russ's thumb.

"Just as they were opening the chute, I heard someone yell, 'Hey, they put a suicide cinch on that guy.' Imagine how I felt. I guess it was the way the guy wrapped the rope around my thumb. But I got through it."

Later he rode a bare-backed bronc named Big Red. "He could buck your arm right out of the socket," Russ recalls, "but it was the most exhilarating experience I'd had up to that time, besides diving off cliffs in Hawaii."

Russ began experimenting with more and more things, most of them quite physical and often very dangerous. But he survived his fling with the rodeo. Then during that summer of 1971, he learned he had been offered an athletic scholarship to the University of Oregon. He jumped at it, and became a freshman at the Eugene, Oregon campus in the fall.

The Oregon Beavers had an exciting team when Russ started his first year there. The club was pass oriented and featured the throwing of Dan Fouts, now a superstar quarterback with the San Diego Chargers, and the catching of Bobby Moore (known today as Ahmad Rashad, the great wide receiver of the Minnesota Vikings). Moore was also the team's best running back. With Russ returning to tight end, there was the prospect of a fine career at Oregon, and the possibility of going on to the pros.

But his scholarship was not only for football. With his cannon-like throwing arm, the baseball team also wanted him, and he was especially coveted in track. Oregon has long been known for its track squad and many outstanding runners often got to Eugene to train. By the time Russ entered Oregon he was throwing the javelin around 265 feet consistently and had thrown close to 275 feet, making him one of the better throwers in the entire world at that time. So there were high hopes of making him an Olympic thrower by the next summer.

He played freshman football as a tight end and quickly showed he had varsity potential. But once the season ended, he began to concentrate on the javelin since the Olympic trials were early in the summer. But that's when he ran into problems, creating a situation that Russ still calls "perhaps the biggest disappointment of my life."

"Since I had thrown 275 feet already and felt I was getting better rapidly, I thought I had a great chance to make the U.S. Olympic team, and perhaps take a medal. The coach at Oregon, Bill Bowerman, said he also felt I could make the team, but if I wanted a chance to take the gold I'd have to make some changes in my style of throwing.

"So they began to play with my style, and in a nutshell, it ruined me. Changing throwing styles caused me to hurt my arm, I guess like a baseball pitcher who alters his delivery. Anyway, I never could throw again like I had before. I remember one meet where I was even *under* 200 feet. It was as bad as that. I used to throw 240 just standing still.

"After that I kept changing my style trying to find the secret again. But I just couldn't get it back. I went to the Olympic trials and finished fifth, or something like that. Naturally, I didn't make the team. It still bothers me and always will. When I came to Oregon I was ranked third in the country. I still like the coach. He's a nice guy. But I know if I hadn't changed my style I would have been in the Olympics."

His chances at the Olympics over, Russ returned the following year with a renewed desire to play football. He felt he had a good chance to start. He had filled out and was an imposing physical specimen at tight end. Indeed, Russ did win a starting job. Then in the second game of the season against Oklahoma, as Oregon was getting throttled by an unimaginable 68-3 score, Russ broke his ankle. He was through for the year.

It was the first time the injury jinx had struck him but it wouldn't be the last. The longer anyone plays, the more chance of pain and injury. Russ could play with the pain, as can most of the great ones, but no one plays with a broken ankle. He was terribly disappointed.

Of course, Russ was not one to waste time. While he was rehabilitating the ankle, he plunged deeper into his schoolwork, studying animal science and maintaining a B average. Then when the next season rolled around he was ready. He won the tight end spot on an Oregon team that was more or less an also-ran in the Pacific-Eight Conference.

But, as usual, Russ Francis was impressive. As a 240-lb. tight end he was a devastating blocker. On another play he could come off the line like a wide receiver and make the play either in the open field or in heavy traffic. And he seemed to do it all with relative ease. But, for some reason, his easy way of doing things often got him in trouble, even then.

But others saw the big guy as a potential star One of them was Mike Hickey, still a pro scout today. He saw Russ and his Oregon team play against the Air Force Academy in 1973.

"It was like watching and all-pro guard play against a kid in the Pop Warner League," Hickey recalls. "Russ simply overpowered everyone who got in his way. I was amazed."

Russ continued to play outstanding football all year long. When the season ended, he was the third ranking Pac-8 receiver with 31 catches for 495 yards. He was named to the All-Conference team and even showed up on a couple of the All-America teams, either as second team or honorable mention. Not bad for an unheralded performer who saw no real action until his junior year. And like with all his other physical endeavors, Russ liked to look for perfection, and at the pure form of the various skills involved.

"I like the concentration of football," he said. "For instance, when you go out for a pass you first must concentrate fully on the pass route. Then you've got to concentrate completely on the ball, and catching it. When you catch it, you switch your concentration completely to running. And I like contact. In fact, sometimes when there's an interception I find I'm almost glad, because it gives me a chance to make a tackle. Same thing when I'm blocking. If everything goes perfectly and my block springs a back for a touchdown, it's a great feeling."

Since Russ had come through his junior year relatively free of injuries, save the usual bumps and bruises picked up in the weekly battles, he decided to try something else. He went out for baseball in the spring and quickly became one of the stalwarts of the Oregon pitching staff. In fact, it wasn't long before his blazing fastball was attracting a number of major league scouts to Eugene when the big guy was on the mound.

So it looked as if Russ was finally in the driver's seat. He'd be returning to Oregon for his senior year in 1974 as an established tight end with vast potential. People were already predicting that another strong season and he was a potential number one draft choice in the NFL. Plus he had an alternative. His live right arm led many to predict he could make it to the major leagues as a pitcher with just a little bit more experience.

But just when things seemed to falling into the right places, Russ Francis again showed just what a high principled and tough-minded individual he was. The powers that be at Oregon decided the football program needed new direction and fired head coach Dick Enright. It's something that happens in all sports. The team isn't going well and the coach is dumped. Most times, whether they like it or not, the players remain and begin working with the new man.

Not Russ Francis. He had liked the coach very

much and didn't approve of the manner in which the whole thing was handled. He decided he didn't want to continue in a program that would treat a man that way. He announced he wouldn't be playing football in 1974, and a short time later decided to leave school altogether.

"Coach Enright got a bad deal and it really upset me," Russ explained. "I don't like to do anything unless I'm happy with it, and I wouldn't have been happy playing football my senior year under those circumstances. That's just the way I am."

So it was good-bye to Oregon, and to many, so long to chances of being drafted near the top a year later. Because of the NCAA rules, Russ still had to wait until his class graduated before playing pro ball. But that didn't stop the Kansas City Royals of the American League from drafting Russ as a pitching prospect. He could have signed with them right there and tried his hand at baseball. But he said no. In fact, getting tabbed in the baseball draft made Russ realize something that must have been churning in his subconscious for a long while.

"I didn't really have much of a decision to make when I heard about the Kansas City draft," he says. "For I realized then that deep down inside I had always wanted to play pro football."

Russ didn't exactly remain idle during what would have been the 1974 football season. For one thing, he joined his father in the sometimes carnival atmosphere known as the pro wrestling circuit. For Russ, it was amusing and fun.

"Fun and some pin money," he conceded. "Dad, of course, had been wrestling and promoting for a long time. He wasn't wrestling as much anymore, but I guess he figured it would be an experience to be in there with one of his sons. So he and I were paired in some tag-team matches and we both had a lot of fun. And to make it even better, we won most of our matches. Not bad.''

That wasn't all Russ did. He decided to indulge himself and follow-up on another long-time passion—flying. He began taking lessons, learned fast as usual, and acquired his pilot's license in the amazing time of just three weeks. And he was barely twenty-one years of age.

Meanwhile, another football season was just about gone and many of the top collegiate players were busy building their reputations and impressing the pro scouts. But in what would have been his senior year, Russ Francis was taking flying lessons and working as a professional wrestler. In reality, he had played just one full season of college ball. It seemed most unlikely that he would be a high choice of any of the NFL teams.

Yet one team was still very much interested in Russ. The New England Patriots were coached by Chuck Fairbanks, who had previously coached at Oklahoma. Fairbanks got a glimpse of Russ back in 1972, in the very game in which Russ broke his ankle. But he recalled being impressed by his size and speed, and was well aware of the fine year the big tight end had in '73, even though Fairbanks had moved on to the pros by then. So when the Pats began thinking about the 1974 college draft, Fairbanks sent scout Dick Steinberg to find out if Russ had kept himself in shape despite his lay-off from the game.

When Steinberg found Russ, the big guy was certainly willing to work out for him. Russ had no football shoes with him and Steinberg said that was too bad, because he had hoped Russ would run a forty-yard dash. Forty yards is the distance a team uses to judge a player's speed. Without hesitation, Russ said he'd run it anyway, took off his street shoes, and got ready to go in his bare feet.

"I didn't think I could get a true reading that way," Steinberg recalls. "If anything, it would be slower in the bare feet. But I figured I might as well let him run just to get a rough idea of his speed."

At Steinberg's signal, Russ took off, and flashed across the finish line in 4.7 seconds. Steinberg couldn't believe his stopwatch.

"All the time he was telling me that he was out of shape and probably couldn't run a true 40 because he had no shoes," the scout remembers. Then he comes in with that time which was just incredible for a big guy in bare feet. I thought I read the watch wrong and I asked him to do it again.

"So he went again and gave me another 4.7 clocking. I knew right then and there that there was nothing wrong with his feet or his attitude. A lot of guys wouldn't have run without the right shoes figured a slow clocking might hurt their chances of being picked high. But there was no feeling like that with Russ."

The Patriots didn't want to make a mistake. They felt they were building a solid club again after a number of down seasons. Though they needed a tight end, the fact still remained that Russ's college credentials were rather incomplete. Should they draft him high or wait, and hope he was still available on a lower round?

The team had been an original American Football League franchise when that league was formed to rival the NFL in 1960. They were known as the

Boston Patriots then and one of the better teams in the early days of the AFL. In fact, they got into the title game in 1963, but lost it to the San Diego Chargers. The club stayed a winner through 1966, then began to fade.

There was a 3-10-1 season in 1967, and then a couple of 4-10 years. By the time the two leagues completed their merger in 1970, the Patriots came into the NFL and promptly posted a 2-12 mark. They were now one of the poorer teams in the entire league. The following year the club was renamed the New England Patriots and were playing in a new park, Schaefer Stadium in Foxboro, Massachusetts.

Then in 1973 came a new coach, Chuck Fairbanks, who had a highly successful career at Oklahoma. His job was simple: rebuild the Patriots and make the team a winner. The team had drafted a Heisman Trophy-winning quarterback, Jim Plunkett, out of Stanford in 1971, and Plunkett produced a fine rookie season, rallying the Pats to a 6-8 mark. But in '72, the team fell back to 3-11, and that's the club Fairbanks was inheriting.

Fairbanks moved quickly to build a nucleus, in both lines and at the so-called skill positions. The 1973 draft brought fullback Sam Cunningham, wide receiver Darryl Stingley, guard John Hannah, and linebacker Sugar Bear Hamilton. An offensive tackle, Leon Gray, was picked up on waivers from Miami. All these players would contribute significantly to the rise of the Patriots over the next several season.

But in 1973, the team managed just a 5-9 mark. Yet it was progress. The first year players performed well and picked up valuable experience.

Then in the 1974 draft came linebacker Steve Nelson, halfback Andy Johnson, and linebacker Sam Hunt. The club also picked up an accurate leftfooted placekicker, John Smith, a former British soccer player who came in as a free agent. And it all worked out to the tune of a .500 season, the club finishing at 7-7.

So by 1975 Coach Fairbanks and his staff felt the team had a great shot at a winning season. In the draft they wanted to try to tie up some loose ends and also begin adding much-needed depth to the team. Perhaps their biggest gamble came on the first round. It certainly surprised many of the other teams in the league to pick a guy with so little college experience but the Pats made Russ Francis their top pick in the 1975 draft.

They got some other good ones, too, like linebacker Rod Shoate from Oklahoma, and quarterback Steve Grogan of Kansas State. There seemed to be a real feeling in the air that the Pats were beginning to build something very solid. Of course, their top choice was something of an unknown quantity. The team even tried to use this approach in contract negotiations with Russ, telling him, in effect, hey, we're taking a chance with you. And they quickly learned they weren't dealing with an ordinary, timid rookie.

"I told them very simply, if you're taking a chance, why did you draft me on the first round," Russ recalls.

So much for leverage. Russ sooned signed what he felt was a fair contract and began preparing for his first season in the pros. He wasn't at all intimidated by the prospect of it all. He simply felt he could play with the big boys and he gave that impression to those around him. As Pats president Bob Marr said of the rookie:

"Confidence is not Russ's problem."

That didn't mean there weren't some rough moments in training camp. After two particularly hard workouts on a very hot day, Russ fell asleep during the team meeting that night and really got the riot act read to him by Coach Fairbanks.

"The coach has a certain way of letting you know something," Russ said. "Without saying it in words, he made it clear that if it happened again I'd probably be playing somewhere else."

Confident though he was, Russ wasn't naive. He knew there was a great deal to learn, especially since he had played just the one full year in college. And it wasn't long before he felt very good about winding up with the Patriots.

"I knew there was a great deal I didn't know and felt lucky to be working with Coach Fairbanks and the rest of his staff," Russ recalls. "I was really fond of the Pats' receiver's coach then, Ray Perkins. I made the mistake of telling him my first year that if he ever saw me do anything wrong on the practice field or in a game, to get on my back about it. So he stayed on my back for a couple of years.

"But Ray was the one who taught me how to block and how to do a lot of the little things that you have to know to survive in this league. It's funny, once I hit training camp and began scrimmaging, then moved into the preseason games, I knew I could play up here. But you still have to know the little things, and having someone like Ray teach them to you avoids a great deal of painful on-the-job lessons."

By the end of the preseason it was increasingly

obvious that Russ had won a starting job. He would be playing a position that had been in something of a transition for the past ten or twelve years. There was a time in the early days that the tight end was little more than an interior lineman. So he had to be big and strong, and able to block tackles and ends, and sometimes linebackers.

When teams began throwing more and using more complex formations, the tight end began catching more passes. But he was still used mainly as a safety valve, an emergency receiver who didn't go deep. He was thrown to mainly when the wide receivers and backs were covered. And there might be a few short-yardage plays designed especially for him.

But in the 1970s, with the advent of the zone defense and other complex coverages, not to mention the faster, quicker linebackers and defenses backs, the tight end had become an integral part of the passing attack. So now the ideal tight end still had to be able to do the heavy-duty blocking and catch the short ones, but it was an invaluable bonus if he could also go deep, catch in a crowd, and run with the ball once he had it. Russ Francis gave every indication of being able to do all these things, and that's why the Pats were so high on him as the 1975 season was set to begin.

The team seemed to be coming in on a high note of optimism. But late in the preseason they suffered a blow when quarterback Plunkett suffered a shoulder separation and would miss several games of the regular season. This left the club almost empty at the crucial signal-calling position. There was the inexperienced Neil Graff and rookie Steve Grogan.

Graff got the call in the opener against Houston and couldn't move the club. Grogan got a shot in the final session and showed some passing potential, but the team was shut out. In his first game, Russ played well, especially on his blocking assignments. He also seemed to know what he was doing on his passing routes and didn't have the timidity of many rookies.

The next week the club lost to Miami, 22-14, blowing a 14-0 lead in the process. But Russ played well again and made several good catches. The tight end job was his to keep, if he could. The big problem now was getting the team straightened out. Plunkett returned against the Jets the following week, but was ineffective. So was Grogan, and the Pats were buried, 36-0. From that promising 7-7 season of '74, they were suddenly 0-3 and fading fast.

Another loss followed before the Pats finally won a game, beating Baltimore, 21-10. The next week Plunkett was hurt again. Young Grogan replaced him with the score 3-0, Pats, and led the club to a 24-16 victory over San Francisco. Perhaps the club had found themselves a good, young quarterback. Grogan had certainly been impressive, as had Russ, who continued to play very well and now was beginning to catch more passes. In fact, his per catch average was climbing above the mid-teens, showing his ability to go deep and hang onto the ball.

The Pats lost to St. Louis the following week and in that game Russ began to feel the pain of playing in the NFL. He had blocked his man on a rushing play and was on the ground when halfback Leon McQuay, carrying the ball, ran into him and either kicked him or hit him with his knee in the back of the neck.

"I saw him coming but couldn't get out of the way," Russ recalls. "I didn't lose consciousness, but I sure lost my senses. It was a strange feeling. Both my vision and speech blurred and I lost my sense of smell and taste. When I got to the sidelines Jim Plunkett asked if I was all right and later told me I didn't make much sense."

Russ returned to the game and was ready to go full speed again the following week. And he seemed to have a philosophical attitude about the heavy contact and violence of the pro game.

"What happened to me was obviously an accident and wasn't personal. In fact, the guy that did it was on my own team. And with other teams, I don't really care who I knock down. I remember when we played the Steelers later that year there was a lot of talk on the line. Guys were saying things like, 'Hey, rookie, we're gonna get you. Hey, rookie, you're holding. Watch out, you. . . . Stuff like that. But I never answer them. I'm out there to block, not to talk."

So the season continued. Rookie Grogan was now the quarterback and rookie Francis was one of his primary receivers. The team seemed to find itself with a solid, 33-19, victory over San Diego. In that game Russ missed one pass which Grogan fired very hard at him. "I shouldda had it," he said. "It's a matter of touch and this is a learning experience. That's the only way to look at it."

As for Grogan, he seemed to have enormous potential. He had a strong arm and could run out of the pocket. On one play in the San Diego game Russ was wide open in the end zone and Grogan overthrew him. Now it was the quarterback's turn to explain.

"I made mistakes and that was one of them, he said. "I saw Russ open but I got excited and overanxious and I overthrew him. You just hope it doesn't happen too often."

So the team was at 3-5, but at least there was a chance to salvage the season, maybe still finish above .500. Russ was optimistic about it, as were many of his teammates. But in the ensuing weeks things just seemed to go sour, more so with the defense than with the offense. In fact, the offense put some real good numbers on the board.

Against the Doomsday Defense of the Dallas Cowboys, they racked up 31, but the club lost, 33-31. At Buffalo, Grogan set a club record with 25 completions and the offense racked up a team mark of 498 yards. Yet the defense was nearly non-existent as Buffalo won, 45-31.

In that game, Russ had his best day as a pro. He grabbed seven of Grogan's passes for 125 yards and one score. He was a real force, and for the first time people around the NFL began to realize that the Pats might have gotten themselves a real gem on the first round. In fact, those seven catches in the Buffalo game still represent the most catches Russ has made in a single contest.

The only problem was that the team continued to lose. Miami beat them, then the Jets, Buffalo again, and finally the Baltimore Colts. Six straight losses, tumbling the Pats back into the AFC Eastern Division basement with an embarrassing, 3-11, final record. There were some stories of team dissension and problems between players and coaches. To many, the Pats weren't a 3-11 team.

There was just too many good people on the club.

One of them was definitely Russ Francis. Playing in all fourteen games his rookie year, Russ grabbed 35 passes for 636 yards and four scores. He was the Patriots second ranking receiver and his average of 18.2 yards per catch was more typical of a wide receiver than a tight end. He was named to a number of all-rookie teams and obviously had an unlimited future. He said he thoroughly enjoyed his rookie year and learned a tremendous amount from it. He still wanted to improve in all phases of his game, especially his blocking.

With Russ, the questions always seem to turn philosophical, and sure enough someone asked him if, after a year in the pro game, he thought the sport dehumanizing. He thought a minute.

"I'm part of a working organism," he answered. "The organism is, of course, the team, and you must have a sense that you can't let the team down. As I see it, football is only dehumanizing if you take it too seriously. Once you let the game consume you, then you're in trouble."

So Russ was still the free spirit, even after a great rookie season. That's not the kind of comment coaches like to read or even some teammates care to see. It almost sounds as if the players just doesn't care that much. But Russ also said there was a feeling of not letting the team down, so he was covering all the bases. On thing was for sure. Everyone connected with the Patriots and the NFL would have to get used to Russ saying and doing his own thing in the upcoming seasons.

In fact, he was at it soon after the season ended. He was back on the wrestling circuit for awhile with Dad and brother Billy. He also spent more time in the air with his other passion—flying. And, of course, he was in Hawaii as much as possible where the last thing he thinks about is football.

But the New England braintrust was thinking of nothing else. They wanted to plug the holes in the defense and add more depth to the club. The draft brought a pair of highly-touted defensive backs, Mike Haynes and Tim Fox. Also joining the team for the 1976 season were defensive tackle Richard Bishop and quarterback Tom Owen.

The team made another major move. They traded long-time quarterback Jim Plunkett and gave the starting job to Steve Grogan, who had played so well as a rookie in 1975. And when training camp started, many of the Patriots were determined not to have another disaster such as 1975.

"We were all pretty much ashamed of ourselves when camp started," Russ said. "We were simply disgusted by the way we played in '75 and vowed that it wouldn't happen again."

But the multi-interested Francis doesn't always set a perfect example. The Pats' practice field was in Smithfield, Rhode Island, and near a small airport. And the constant sound of the planes going over drove Russ crazy.

"With all those planes coming right over the field, I really had trouble concentrating," he said. "I just love watching them. So one of the coaches is always tapping me on the shoulder and telling me to get with it. But sometimes my head is up there in the clouds with those planes and I just wish I were up there, too."

How many top athletes would wish they were someplace else during practice? Not many. But not necessarily because they wouldn't want to be somewhere else. Rather, few would have the courage to admit it. Yet when it was time to come out of the chute, Russ Francis was usually ready.

The club opened the 1976 season against the Baltimore Colts and the game seemed to mirror much of the action of the previous year. The offense moved the ball well, but the defense was throttled by Baltimore quarterback Bert Jones, who led his club to a 27-13 victory.

But a mirror does not always give an accurate impression. This was not the same Patriot team that went 3-11 in '75. A week later they turned it around and whipped the Miami Dolphins, a very solid team, 30-14. Now they had a date with the two-time Super Bowl champion Pittsburgh Steelers. This would be the real test. The Steelers didn't like to lose to anyone.

The first half of the game was poorly played. Neither team seemed to do anything right. The Steelers even fumbled the ball away six times in their own territory during the first two periods alone. Yet the best the Patriot offense could do with all those fumbles was get three field goals from John Smith. Pittsburgh still managed enough firepower to take a 13-9 lead into the lockerroom at the half.

When Pittsburgh got another touchdown early in the third period it looked as if the Pats were done. Then, without warning, the New England offense began coming alive. The offensive line began giving Steve Grogan more protection and he was connecting with his receivers. And big Russ Francis began to run wild in the vaunted Steeler secondary. Whenever the Pats were in a hole it seemed that Grogan wanted to go to Russ.

At one point in the third period New England had the ball on its own seven. Pittsburgh put on the big rush and Grogan found himself scrambling for his life in the end zone. But he spotted Russ free and hit the big guy for an 18-yard gain and a key first down. That kept the drive alive and the Pats moved upfield, over the 50, and into Pittsburgh territory.

With the ball at the Steeler 38, Grogan dropped back again. This time he saw Russ streaking down the sideline and hit his tight end for a 38-yard scoring play. Russ had turned on his great speed and caught the Steeler defenders off guard. The kick made it 20-16, and the Pats were back in the game. Minutes later Grogan hit Darryl Stingley for a 58-yard TD play to put his club out in front, 23-20.

In the final period the Pats began moving again. Once more Grogan connected with Russ on the big play of the drive. This time it was a 48-yarder that brought the ball all the way to the Steeler 21. Several plays later the Pats got the clinching score, taking a 30-20 lead, and holding on for perhaps their biggest victory in more than 10 years, 30-27.

The game really marked the coming of age of the entire team, and especially quarterback Grogan and Russ Francis. Grogan now had the confidence that he could throw and win against the best, and Russ showed that no secondary could control him, long or short. In fact, one writer covering the game, had this as part of his story.

" . . . Russ Francis was virtually unstoppable all afternoon. Whoever heard of a tight end grabbing passes of 38 and 48 yards. At 6'-6", 240-pounds he blocks like a tackle or guard, but he can also fly down the sideline like a wide receiver. The man has the potential to be awesome. Correction: he already is. . ."

It was one of Russ's greatest games. He had nabbed six of Grogan's aerials for 139 yards and a score. That's an average of more than 23 yards a catch. No wonder Russ was already being touted as a prototype tight end of the future. He could do it all.

The victory over the Steelers seemed to ignite everyone. A week later they steamrolled a very powerful Oakland Raider team, 48-17. The Patriots were suddenly the surprise team of the entire NFL. Yet not all veteran football men were surprised. Former quarterback George Blanda, a long-time player, put it this way:

"You can't go by the Patriots record last year. You've got to go back to 1974 when they were 7-7. They were a very tough, young football team then, and they've built on the nucleus of players they had that year. Their success doesn't surprise me at all."

What surprised a lot of people was the result the following week. Coming off three big victories against top teams, the Pats found themselves on the short end of a 30-10 score against a very weak Detroit team. It seemed like a natural letdown after the club had ridden such an incredible high. Unfortunately, it would become disturbing pattern over the next few years. The club would win some big, big games, then blow the one that was supposed to be the laugher.

After the Detroit loss they bounced back to topple the New York Jets, 41-7, then whipped Buffalo, 26-22. The club had completed half its schedule with a 5-2 slate and realized for the first time in many years it had a chance to reach the playoffs.

As for Russ, he was having another great year. His overall stats were down somewhat from the season before, but the Pats had a more balanced offense, and now presented one of the most devastating running attacks in the league. But Russ was still impressing people, one of his biggest boosters was Pats receiving coach Ray Perkins.

"The amazing thing is that Russ can run with most wide receivers in the league," said Perkins. "Plus he's very tall, yet flexible, and can run his patterns and cut very well. He's easy to work with, very intelligent, and is going to be a great ballplayer for a long time."

Next came Miami again and out once more emerged the other side of Russ Francis. The game was played in Florida and the warm weather seemed to do something to Russ. For instance, the team went down a few days early to practice there, and the day before the game, one of the coaches found Russ playing tennis with a woman sportswriter. It was a hot day, and Russ was running around the court in his bare feet!

He even asked the coaches if he could stay over an extra night after the game and fly back to Boston the next day. There was also all the time he could get on the warm beaches. So it was no real surprise when both Russ and his teammates played a dull, flat game and lost to the Dolphins, 10-3. Later, Russ admitted he had problems concentrating.

"Man, that sunshine!" he said. "Up in New England it was just starting to get cold and I was homesick for Hawaii. But needless to say, after the game I didn't mention anything more to Coach Fairbanks about staying over an extra night. I didn't dare."

Perhaps the letdown in Miami was just what Russ and the Pats needed. For after that, they went on another tear. First it was Buffalo, 20-10, then an upset win over division-leading Baltimore, 21-14, then 38-24 over the Jets and 39-14 against Denver.

Suddenly they were 9-3 with two games left. It was an incredible turnaround. And when they whipped New Orleans, 27-6, and then beat Tampa Bay, 31-14, they finished at 11-3, tied for first in the AFC East with Baltimore, and they were in the playoffs!

It had been an incredible season for the entire team, with many standout individuals. Quarterback Grogan, fullback Cunningham, wide receiver Stingley were all outstanding. Guard John Hannah and tackle Leon Gray, playing on the left side of the offensive line, were simply awesome. The defense was much improved. With Haynes and Fox in the secondary, teams couldn't pass at will against the Pats any longer. They had become a truly outstanding football team.

Also contributing mightily was Russ Francis. Russ caught 26 passes in 13 games for 367 yards and three scores. His per catch average was 14.1. Though his catching stats were down a bit from his rookie year, the balanced offense didn't dictate he do more. He was actually improved in every facet of his game and his peers recognized it by naming him an all-pro and also picking him to play in the Pro Bowl after the playoffs. He also found himself being compared to Oakland's great tight end, Dave Casper.

"I don't think Russ was the best tight end in football this past year," said Ray Perkins. "Dave Casper was probably more consistent. But Russ is a hard worker and wants to be the best. I think he's already the strongest blocking tight end in the game. In fact, he thinks he is, too. That's another reason he's going to be the best. There's nothing he doesn't think he can do."

There were plenty of people who thought the

Pats were good enough to get to the Super Bowl in 1976. They certainly had the big-play personnel to do it. But their first roadblock wouldn't be easy to overcome. The always-tough, playoff-wise Oakland Raiders. Even though the Pats had rolled over them in the regular season there was no way to predict that they would do it again. In fact, most football people considered the Raiders the favorites.

So the Pats were bucking the odds, including the fact that the game was being played at Oakland. Yet they came out with fire in their eyes and dominated the game early, moving the ball well on offense and stopping quarterback Ken Stabler and the rest of the Raider attack. And the Patriots first score came as the result of another brilliant catch by Russ Francis.

Once again Grogan sent him deep and fired high and long. Racing with the Oakland defenders, Russ reached up with one hand and pulled the ball home for a 40-yard gain. To some, his arm seemed to extend further than possible, but somehow he got the ball. Asked about the catch later, the mystical side of Russ emerged.

"The ball just seemed to slow down and crawl through the air as I came closer to it," he said. "Then as it hit my hand, I looked down and watched it dimple my skin. It's funny, but I sometimes think I can make something happen on the football field by just picturing it in my mind."

At any rate, the catch led to a Patriot score. That seemed to set the tone for the game. Though the Raiders wouldn't quit, the Pats continued to outplay them. By the third period it was still close, with New England leading, 14-10. The Pats had the ball again and Russ went out on a short pattern, maybe 10 yards downfield. He made his cut and turned to look for the ball. That's when the lights went out.

"George Atkinson, the safetyman, just came up and drove his forearm between my mask and the top of the helmet," Russ recalls. "I was really stung. In fact, it felt like a bullet had gone through my head. I reached up to find my nose, but it wasn't there. It was over around my cheek someplace."

Russ kind of staggered to the bench, blood streaming from his nose, which was later found to be broken in three places. But in the heat of a playoff game, you can't always worry about technicalities, like a nose broken in three places.

"What do you think you're doing here?" linebacker Steve Zabel screamed at Russ.

"I think my nose is broken," Russ answered.

"I don't give a hoot about that," Zabel said. "You can't come out of this game. We need you on the field. Get back out there, fast."

"So I told the doctor I wanted to go back in," Russ said. "He gave the nose a couple of yanks and fixed it up a little. But the more he yanked at it the more I figured I was safer in the huddle. So back I went. I really thought for a while that day that maybe I had reached my limit. But the way it turned out, I hadn't."

Russ went back and immediately began blocking like a demon once again. With the ball on the Oakland 26, Russ went in motion outside, Atkinson again guarding him. This time he went downfield, put a move on, and cut across the middle. Grogan got the ball there and Russ lugged it into the end zone for a score. He then calmly flipped it to Atkinson, who was trailing the play, badly beaten.

The TD and extra point made the score 21-10

with about a minute left in the third period. It certainly looked as if the Pats were in the driver's seat. But the Raiders had been in these kinds of games before and they never quit. Early in the final session they scored to cut the New England lead to 21-17. They were like a bunch of vultures lurking around, waiting to pounce on any Patriot mistake.

But the Pats didn't panic. They continued to play sound football, and midway through the period embarked on another drive, one they hoped would eat up a good portion of the clock. With just under six minutes left, the Pats had brought the ball all the way to the Oakland 28. A touchdown would just about ice it, and a field goal would give them a seven-point cushion.

Then came two crucial plays. On second down Grogan dropped back and looked for Russ. Linebacker Phil Villapiano was on him, but Russ had a step on him. Grogan threw, but Russ couldn't catch it because Villapiano had pinned both his arms to his side. Russ looked for a flag. There was none. He couldn't believe it.

"I knew when I went out for that pass," he said, "that unless I dropped it we had ourselves a first down. Then Villapiano grabs me and pins my arms against my sides. No penalty. Later, he told me he was sorry he did it. 'You know, Russ,' he said, 'you got to take chances.' "

The Pats went for it again on the next play, only this time a flag was dropped . . . offside against the Pats. Another controversial call. The ball was brought back to the 33 and then a field goal try was missed. Now Oakland had the ball with a chance to win it.

Cool Kenny Stabler moved his club downfield slowly and methodically, playing the clock, but not rushing. With just 50 seconds remaining and the ball on the New England 27, a third down play, Stabler dropped back and threw an incomplete pass. It looked like the Pats would hold. But wait. Another flag! This one for roughing the passer. The Raiders had a first down on the 13.

They moved in closer, and with just 10 seconds left, scored the touchdown that gave them a 24-21 victory. The Patriots had lost a heartbreaker and were eliminated from the playoffs.

"I was in a state of shock for a few days after that one," Russ admitted. "I didn't even want to think. There was no doubt in my mind that we should have won. In fact, as far as I'm concerned we did beat the Raiders. Only the officials beat us."

Yet even in defeat, Russ had been magnificent. He grabbed four passes for 96 yards and a touchdown, and had played so well with the broken nose. It won him new legions of admirers in high places.

"Russ is one of the best athletes in the league," said Al Davis, the astute owner of the Raiders. "We have nothing but respect for the guy. We have to respect him after the way he played against us."

And Chuck Noll, coach of the Steelers, also joined the club. "Russ is just a special type of football player," said Noll. "To put it simply, he does things out there that no other tight end can do."

So it had been a great year, for both Russ and the Patriots despite the heartbreaking playoff loss. The team completely turned itself around and looked to be contenders for a long time to come. And Russ seemed to be very content with the situation at New England.

"My goal now is to be the best tight end in football and the best paid," he said. "I feel that I'm in the right place to do it. I love playing in New England and with the other guys on this team. We now have one of the best offensive units in football. We've got tough players at every position and other teams can't concentrate on stopping any one guy. We can run and throw with the best, we're young, and we want to win."

Russ also admitted it was difficult leaving Hawaii to return to football each year.

"I always have second thoughts when I have to leave," he said. "I miss the beauty of the place and my friends, people I grew up with. Yet I've grown to love Boston. Of all the cities I've seen, I'm glad I got to play here.

"There are many interesting things to do. I go to the Boston Pops concerts and spend a lot of time at the Museum of Fine Arts. Sometimes I go to Norwood Airport and rent a plane, then fly to either Nantucket or Martha's Vineyard, or maybe some other part of New England.

"Basically, I prefer to be comfortable with my surroundings and the people I'm with. And there are still a lot of things I want to do and see around here."

It looked as if the team was still building. The 1977 draft brought return specialist and defensive back Raymond Clayborn, running back Horace Ivory, and wide receiver Stanley Morgan. Now the club was expected to win and that put more pressure on everyone. Matters weren't helped, either, when the team's two great offensive lineman, John Hannah and Leon Gray, refused to report to training camp. They were holding out as a tandem for new contracts, and many felt their actions broke the harmony that had been built the year before. Both reported, but not until the season was ready to begin, and it took them several games to regain their all-pro form.

Russ came in his usual free-spirited self. He had wrestled again in the off-season, then came into camp with some 200 books he planned to read during the course of the season. There were still people bothered by the image he presented, of a guy who didn't seem to give his whole heart and soul to the game. And he never disappointed when someone asked him about it.

"There's always talk that I'm too easygoing in practice," he said. "But I study the plays and I know them, and I execute them with precision. What I don't do is go around with a frown on my face, and I'm not shopping for a coronary. And, yes, I do goof around in practice. I laugh, hit guys, fall on the ground. And sometimes when a ball is thrown my way I try to catch it with one hand. You know, there are times in a game when I can only use one hand, like in the playoff against Oakland."

That game was still sticking in Russ's craw, as it was with many of his teammates. So they started the 1977 season determined to get back into the playoffs once more. But in the early weeks of the year something new and frustrating began plaguing the team—inconsistency.

After winning the opener from Kansas City, they lost to Cleveland and the New York Jets by identical 30-27 scores. Then came wins of Seattle and San Diego and a big one over Baltimore, 17-3, in which Russ grabbed a 31-yard TD toss from Grogan. Another victory over the Jets seemed to have the team back on track, but suddenly reverses to Buffalo and Miami marred the picture. After nine games the club was just 5-4, and a playoff berth very questionable.

There were some who said that the things that helped make the '76 Pats the surprise team of the league, were now hurting the club. There was too much recklessness, too many interceptions, and an almost predictable letdown against the weaker teams. Still, they had the talent and won against Buffalo, Philadelphia, Atlanta, and Miami, to bring their record up to 9-4.

Now came the big one with Baltimore. If the Pats won, they were in the playoffs, if they lost they were out. It was as simple as that. It was also an important game for Russ Francis. He had not been having a banner year at all. In fact, a rib injury had shelved him for four games and he was just getting back to top shape for the Baltimore contest. So he wanted to do well for more than one reason.

The game was scoreless for one. Then early in the second period the Pats drove downfield and Grogan hit Russ from the five for a touchdown. The big guy was back and the kick made it 7-0. The Colts cut it to 7-3, but New England scored again to make it 14-3 at the half.

A 101-yard kickoff return by Raymond Clayborn was the way the Pats started the second half and suddenly they had a 21-3 lead and seemed well on the way to victory. But the Colts great quarterback, Bert Jones, began rallying his troops. It became a 21-10 game, then 24-10, then after three quarters, 24-16, the Pats still in front.

But in the final session Jones drove his team in again, and the kick made it 24-23. The game was now up for grabs. Suddenly, the Colt defense was controlling the New England offense. The Pats couldn't move, but a great punt put Baltimore on its own one. Jones then began driving the team, converting several crucial third-down situations.

Then a 57-yard completion put the ball deep in New England territory.

With time running out, the Colts moved inside the five. There was a broken play and Jones kept the ball. As he was hit, it squirted loose. A Patriot pounced on it and the New Englanders were going crazy with emotion. They had the ball! But no. The referee ruled he had blown the play dead before the fumble. The ball went back to the Colts.

Television replays clearly showed a fumble. Jones lost the ball before he hit the ground. It was a blown call. And a play later, when Don McCauley carried into the end zone, the blown call had cost the Pats the game and a playoff berth, 30-24.

So for the second straight year, the Patriots season ended with a heartbreaking loss, the outcome helped decidedly by a referee's decision that was wholly open to question. It was not a happy situation. But there were other factors as well. For one thing, Russ played in just 10 games and caught only 16 passes all year for 229 yards and four scores. With that kind of production from a potent force such as Russ, it had to hurt the team. His peers still felt he was one of the best since he was selected to appear in the Pro Bowl for the second straight season.

Football people also pointed to the fact that the Patriot offense scored just 278 points during the '77 season, as opposed to 376 the season before. That difference of nearly 100 points indicated that the offense wasn't nearly as explosive as it had been a year earlier. And for a young team with highly skilled performers, that statistic was difficult to comprehend. For the first time there was a question of intangibles. Was there an attitude problem?

Was it a matter of the chemistry just not being right? Was it the relationship between coaching staff and players? The 1978 season would certain be a crucial test, and there was now more pressure than ever for the team to win.

But before the new season could begin, there was a tragedy of epic proportions. It happened in a pre-season game against the Oakland Raiders. The Pats had the ball and wide receiver Darryl Stingley ran a crossing pattern over the middle. Grogan's pass was slightly overthrown and Stingley lunged for it. At that precise second, he was hit hard by Raider safety Jack Tatum, who had been racing toward him at full speed. Stingley crumbled to the ground instantly and didn't move.

It was a nightmarish scene. First the trainer went out, then a doctor, then more doctors, finally a stretcher. And, still, the young receiver wasn't moving. He was taken from the field and to a hospital. There, the news was bad. Stingley has suffered a broken neck and was paralyzed. The prognosis was pessimistic. He would probably never walk again.

The entire Patriot team was in a state of shock and gloom. Of course, the worse part was the personal tragedy to Stingley. It was a freak accident, a clean, hard hit just in the right spot to do that kind of damage. And it also began to give those around the club an eerie feeling that perhaps this team was snake-bit, that something was always going to happen to them.

Quarterback Grogan took the Stingley tragedy especially hard since he had thrown the ball which the receiver was reaching for when he was hit. The QB had also been under fire because of his inconsistency and charges that he ran with the ball too much. And there were criticism of both Grogan and Coach Fairbanks for the way the team had been utilizing the talents of Russ Francis. To most observers, Russ was a force, a real offensive weapon, and for him to catch just 26 and 16 passes the past two seasons was ridiculous. But Russ defended his coach and quarterback.

"If Steve Grogan was a jerk or didn't know what he was doing, then I might have to say to the coach, 'Hey, let me help the team out and catch a few balls.' But I wasn't unhappy with the way things were. The team was going pretty well and we were certainly competitive with anyone. A couple of breaks here and there and we would have gone even further."

So the Pats went into 1978 as one of the favorites to wind up in the playoffs and maybe the Super Bowl. After Stingley's injury the club traded for veteran wide receiver Harold Jackson, immediately filling that gap. So they still looked quite formidable offensively all the way down the line. It was the first year of the new, 16-game schedule, so it would be a long grind to the playoffs.

The team didn't get off fast, losing two of their first three, with quarterback Grogan again taking a lot of heat. But one thing was very noticeable. Russ was a more integral part of the passing offense then he had been the past two season. He was being thrown to often, and if it was catchable, he'd get it.

Then on September 24, the Pats had another meeting with the Oakland Raiders. Because of the Stingley injury in pre-season, there was a great deal of emotion riding on the game. Both clubs wanted it badly, but the Pats firepower prevailed, and they won a hard-fought, 21-14, decision.

One of the prime movers in the victory was Russ.

He was the man Grogan went to in the big situations, and he responded with five catches for 126 yards and a touchdown. He had one catch of 53 yards and his average for the day was 25 yards a grab. It showed once more just how explosive and intimidating he could be. And when he wasn't catching, he was blocking extremely well.

The Oakland victory started the team on a real roll. They whipped San Diego, Philadelphia, Cincinnati, and Miami, giving them five straight and a 6-2 mark at the halfway point of the season. But the team still showed that tendency for the sudden and unexpected letdown. Leading the tough Houston Oilers, 23-0, late in the second period the following week, they somehow managed to lose the game, 26-23.

But again they righted themselves and played well the second half of the season. In game fifteen, they beat Buffalo, 26-24, to up their record to 11-4, with one game remaining. Yet they had already clinched their first AFC East title and seemed primed and ready for the playoffs. Then, another bombshell struck the team.

It was announced without warning that Coach Fairbanks had accepted an offer to take the head coaching job at the University of Colorado for the 1979 season. For the story to break at this point in the season was bad enough, but that wasn't all. Patriot owner Billy Sullivan suspected that Fairbanks was already at work recruiting for Colorado and neglecting his duties with the Patriots. Just hours before the season finale with Miami, Sullivan went down to the locker room, told Fairbanks to leave, and announced that the coach was being suspended. Assistant coaches Ron Erhardt and Hank Bullough would run the team in the finale.

With the players completely bewildered by the sudden turn of events, they took the field and just went through the motions, losing to the Dolphins, 23-3. And after the game the talk wasn't about the playoffs, but about the Fairbanks situation. Some players felt Fairbanks should be allowed to stay through the post-season, others felt he had betrayed them and should be out. Either way, it was hard to see how the club could regroup and be ready for their first playoff game against the Houston Oilers.

With the team in turmoil once more, statistics really didn't mean much. But for the record, Russ Francis had an outstanding season. He caught a career high 39 passes for 543 yards and four scores. He had missed one game due to injury, but for the first time since he joined the Patriots, he was their leading receiver. He also received all-pro recognition once again and was chosen to play in the Pro Bowl for the third straight year. He seemed to be finally fulfilling all that great potential people had been hearing about since his rookie year.

But the big focus was on the playoffs and the coaching situation. Sullivan made the next move. Four days after suspending Fairbanks, the owner reinstated him, but just for the playoffs. It was a foregone conclusion that he wouldn't be coaching the Pats in 1979. Most of the players and coaches tried to soft-soap the situation, claiming it wouldn't affect the team on the field. But as one player remarked, tongue in cheek:

"This is one big happy family. Now we're going to go upstairs and have a party. Maybe someone will give Chuck a Colorado T-shirt!"

So there was tension, and once the game with Houston started, it was obvious that the Patriots were not a confident, loose, and ready team. Neither team scored in the opening session, but early in the second period Houston's Dan Pastorini tossed a 71-yard TD pass to Ken Burrough and the kick made it a 7-0 game.

That was the beginning. Midway through the period the Oilers went to work again, this time on a methodical, 14-play, 99-yard drive which resulted in another score. They had pushed the Patroit defense the length of the field and led, 14-0. And when Pastorini hit Mike Barber with the TD pass with less than 30 seconds left in the half, it was all but over. The Oilers led, 21-0.

With quarterback Grogan's knee hurting, Tom Owen played the second half and rallied the club to a 24-14 game at one point. But the Oilers took over again and closed it out at 31-14. The Pats were eliminated once more, and this time there were no close calls by the officials to cite. They just played badly.

It was the end of a frustrating season which had more than its share of ups and downs. The Stingley injury started it, then there was the winning streak and division title. Finally, the Fairbanks fiasco and playoff loss. And it was hard to say whether the team could survive emotionally and be an effective unit again. There were already whispers. As one NFL coach put it:

"There's a missing element there somewhere, and it could be character."

As for Russ, he had kept a pretty low profile through the season-ending fiasco. He had to be pleased with his own performance and the fact that during the season he had come to terms with the Patriots on a new, six-year pact which made him one of the best paid players at his position in the league. Around the league he now had the reputation as one of the two best tight ends around (Dave Casper was the other), and perhaps the best blocker at his position. But, characteristically, he always refused to get into a position of making comparisons between himself and anyone else.

"Let's just put it this way," he said, on more than one occasion. "I think Dave Casper is one of the great tight ends in the game and it's nice to be considered in that class. But we're different types of players and any comparison is silly."

But with the season over for the Pats, Russ wanted to do his usual thing—get as far away from football as possible. He still had the Pro Bowl the end of January, but felt he needed a few weeks back home in Hawaii. So back he went to spend some time with his friends, having fun and relaxing. But this time the trip back almost cost him his career . . . and could have cost him a lot more.

He was riding his motorcycle toward the beach with a girlfriend sitting behind him. There was a car riding to his right and the driver suddenly made a left turn without warning. It hit the back of the bike. Russ picks up the story.

"When I saw he was going to run us down from behind I knew we could be killed instantly," he said. "So I swerved the other way trying to cut across in front of him. But he hit the back of the bike and struck Jennifer's (the girl with him) leg. The impact also made the bike speed up toward the side of the road.

"I didn't want to go down on the pavement so I struggled to keep the bike up to reach a grassy area. But there was a cement drainage ditch there and we were going for that head first. So I just jumped off the bike as far as I could to try to clear the ditch. My upper body went over the ditch and I hit some soft grass head first, which probably saved my life. Jennifer still had her arms around me and landed on top of me. The bike hit the cement and some people who saw it said it did three flips before flying to pieces. If we had stayed on it, that would have been us flying to pieces."

As it was, it was a very bad accident. Russ had a severe concussion that kept him unconscious for nearly two days. He also had a broken left hand, a cracked right wrist, a compound fracture of the left ankle, and a badly gashed right foot. Jennifer had a badly broken leg. Though Russ's injuries were serious, the doctors said there would be no permanent damage and that he should be ready to play football on schedule in the summer of 1979 when training camp began. Russ's first reaction when he awakened was more basic.

"I'm just lucky to be alive," he said. "Right now I don't care about the other things. I'm still here and that's all that counts."

A couple of months later, when he was well on the way to recovery, he described the strange reactions he had seconds after the crash and before he lost consciousness.

"My first thought after I knew I was alive was of Darryl (Stingley)," Russ said, "and I wondered if the same thing had happened to me. So I rolled my neck around and I could move it. Then I rubbed my fingers together and knew I could feel them. Then I moved my toes. Jennifer was on the ground beside me. I told her to do the same things. She said she could, and that was the last thing I remembered for the next two days."

Russ was in the hospital for eight days and in a wheelchair for a month more. Then he began rehabilitating his injuries to get ready for the season. It wasn't the way he liked to spend his free time, but it was certainly a necessity. By the second week in July, with training camp just a week away, Russ was pretty much ready to go. He sounded confident.

"I'd say I've been all right for the past two months," he told a Boston reporter. "The ankle was my biggest worry as far as playing again. But it has really been fine and I don't see any problem at all."

When asked if he'd been working out, he gave a typical Russ Francis answer.

"Sure, I've been working out," he said. "Mostly surfing, scuba diving, and sky diving. The surfing and scuba diving are good for your cardiovascular system. As for the sky diving—and maybe I shouldn't be telling Billy Sullivan about this—I figure it's good for your mental toughness."

So Russ hadn't really changed, despite his close call. But then again, no one really expected he would. The big question was whether the team would change. The talent was still there. Ron Erhardt was the new coach and there were more predictions of division titles and a run at the Super Bowl. Even Russ said:

"There's been a lot of turmoil here the past few years, but I've got a good feeling about this team. I think we're gonna surprise a few people."

At the outset of the season both the Patriots and Russ looked very strong. Showing no effects from his motorcycle accident, Russ grabbed five passes in the opener against the Steelers and another five the following week against the Jets. Once again the Pats seemed to have one of the most explosive offensive machines in the league. Russ grabbed five more in the fifth game against Green Bay and was up among the conference leaders.

Then, about the third week in October with the team leading the division with a 5-2 mark and Russ having grabbed 25 passes in those seven games, a story hit the stands that caused the first ruffle in Patriot land. It was a story about all-pro John Hannah in a national magazine, and in the story, Hannah took some shots at his teammate, Russ Francis.

The story quoted Hannah as saying, "But here's a guy with more talent in his finger than I got in my whole body who doesn't use it. If Russ would bust his hump, nobody would know who Dave Casper *was*. But he doesn't. I get upset when I see that kind of thing around here. I want to win so damn much. . ."

There were waves throughout the team when the story broke. Hannah said the quotes weren't exactly accurate, then repeated what he meant to the *Boston Globe,* but it didn't sound much different.

"What I said was that Russ had more ability than I do and that, if he humped his butt, he'd be the best in the NFL," Hannah said. "Russ has got more ability than anybody I've ever seen in the NFL or, for that matter, any other athlete I've ever seen. I didn't mean anything in a derogatory sense."

But it still seemed that he was saying that Russ didn't put out fully at all times and that he wasn't utilizing his great talents. It also implied Russ was part of the attitude problem on the Pats and perhaps the reason the team always came up short. Naturally, Russ felt compelled to answer.

At first, he simply said he felt he was having his best season blocking and receiving, and added, "and if I'm not supposed to try, then why have I been playing when hurt this season? I haven't been able to sleep two nights this week because of the pain."

Russ had bruised hands, a bruised shoulder and bad leg at the time. Later, with more time to reflect, he spoke again about the charges Hannah had made.

"I was a little surprised when I found out what he had said. I was playing hurt at the time, but I don't normally talk about that. Everybody plays hurt, including John. He's just a very intense guy. In fact, I feel very sorry for the guys who line up across from him, even in practice, because he's the only guy out there who puts out 100 percent all the time. But John and I are very different people with a different idea of living.

"Because of this, people view Russ Francis as being unconcerned or not spending the proper time thinking about football. But I take out what I have to learn from every game, then I leave it behind me. Because I don't always say anything after a game people sometimes think I'm not very dedicated. But a loss affects me more than anyone will ever know."

Case closed. Russ then went out and grabbed four more passes in a 28-13 victory over the Dolphins. That gave the club a 6-2 mark at the halfway point and they seemed on their way to the division crown. Russ now had 29 catches and five TD's after eight games and was also on his way to a super year. His new coach, Ron Erhardt, couldn't say enough about him.

"If you've got tight ends who can do the same things as your wide receivers, you're just more flexible," the coach said. "Russ gets deep quick and can run after the catch. He really got his reputation as a great blocker and deep threat. Before this year his reputation as a receiver has always been average at best. Now he's proving he's great at everything."

There was one problem. Russ had been kicked in the back during the Miami game, and afterward it was revealed that he had fractured a small bone there. He would be out for at least two games.

To many, Russ's injury signalled the beginning of the team's demise. Without the big guy and also without fullback Sam Cunningham, the club lost to Baltimore, 31-26, the following week. After that they just weren't the same team. They won the next week without Russ, and then he returned to play part-time against Denver. His back was still so painful that he had trouble getting down in a three-point stance. And when the team was blown out, 45-10, he felt even worse.

Though he remained in action the next three weeks, he wasn't the same player he had been in the first half. The team was on the brink of blowing the division and a playoff shot. Then came another big game with Miami, the team threatening to take the division lead.

The Dolphins were just not the good luck team for Russ in 1979. In the first game he had hurt his back. This time, the game was still up for grabs when the Patriots drove deep into Dolphin territory in the third period. Quarterback Grogan sent Russ toward the goal line and threw. The ball was high and Russ made a desperation dive. He landed head first, and knocked himself out cold. He had to be taken from the field on a stretcher with a severe concussion. His season was over.

Miami ended up winning the game, 39-24, all but

putting a lock on the division crown. The following week they wrapped it up with another win so it didn't matter what the Pats did. Russ wanted to play in the final meaningless game, but the doctors wouldn't let him.

For the Patriots, it was another disaster. After going 6-2 the first half of the year, they limped home at 3-5 over the final eight games to finish with a 9-7 slate, a game behind the Dolphins. They also failed to win one of the two wild card berths in the AFC. Houston and Denver took those with 11-5 and 10-6 records respectively. So the Pats were out of the playoffs again.

It was a very discouraging situation for Russ and his teammates. After 29 catches the first half, injuries limited the big guy to just 10 more the rest of the way. It still equalled his career best of 39 and he gained 557 yards with five TD's. But all those scores came in the first eight games.

As was his practice, Russ enjoyed the off-season and didn't worry about the team's problems. Instead, he indulged in a new passion—sky diving. Simply put, that's jumping out of an airplane and free falling for a short period before opening a parachute and floating to earth. Yes, it can be a very dangerous sport. Many mishaps can occur, including parachutes that fail to open.

The Patriots, of course, weren't thrilled about Russ doing this, but by now they knew their man. In fact, after the motorcycle accident, someone asked Coach Erhardt if the team would ban motorcycles for Russ. He answered at the time:

"If you don't let a guy like Russ ride motorcycles, he's just going to jump out of parachutes or something even worse."

How right the coach had been. Russ's instructor,

Mike Gennis, a two-time member of the world-champion U.S. skydiving team, said his newest pupil was an exceptionally fast learner.

"I don't mind him picking up skydiving," Gennis joked, "but what makes me mad is he's so good at it. It took me two years to get to where he is right now."

A typical jump saw Gennis and Russ leap out of a helicopter at about 6,500 feet. They would free-fall for about 25 seconds, flying to each other, touching hands in midair, and maybe doing a few other maneuvers. Then at 2,500 feet they would open their chutes and fall to earth. Russ loved it.

"I don't care what anybody says," Russ crowed, "catching a touchdown pass, playing in the Pro Bowl, playing in a Super Bowl—which I've never done—but I don't care what you name, skydiving is a thrill that beats all."

There are undoubtedly many people who feel by now that Russ is a reckless daredevil, constantly taking his life in his hands. But an old friend from Hawaii, Colby Jones, disagrees.

"I've never seen Russ do anything that a prudent man wouldn't do," Jones said. "I've flown with him, sailed with him, drunk with him, and I can honestly say that the craziest thing I have ever seen him do is play football. Even the motorcycle accident was just an accident. He wasn't fooling around or out for a Sunday ride. He was just going somewhere."

Indeed, there was a great deal of truth to that. With all the things Russ had done in his life, football had definitely caused him the most pain and most broken bones. As he began looking at 1980, all the accumulated hurts were on his mind.

"I don't worry any more about being the best

this or best that," he said. "No matter what you do, somebody will come along who does it better. My goal is to get out of football healthy and in one piece—and, of course, to play in the Super Bowl. I'm going into this season with the same hopes I've had the last several years. We know we can play with anyone on any given day. So if it's in the stars, we'll be in the Super Bowl."

When Russ rolled into the Pats camp his enthusiasm continued to rise, though it was obvious the injuries he suffered in '79 were still on his mind.

"I think this year we'll finally become the team people have expected us to be. I sense something here. There seems to be more excitement among the players about the coming season, more intensity about playing the game. Maybe this is what we lacked.

"If we don't get wrecked by injuries and screwed up with contract problems, then we should go all the way. I've never said that before since I'm not the kind of guy to make predictions. But a lot of the guys are disappointed about the way the team has played the last few years and we want to play up to our potential this year.

"As for my injuries, well, the tests show that I should be OK. But with head injuries you never really know until you get hit hard again. Until that point, I'll be a little apprehensive."

But there were problems. The team picked up some good draft picks, like running back Vagas Ferguson from Notre Dame, but perennial stars Sam Cunningham and safety Mike Haynes were holding out for new contracts. Plus the team had traded tackle Leon Gray to Houston the year before and some felt that threw off the timing and balance of the offensive line.

The Patriots were again favored to win their division, and when they blew out a good Cleveland team, 34-17, in the opener, things looked very bright. But to skeptics, this had all happened before, so they weren't getting excited early. Russ had just one catch in the Cleveland game, but had to leave with a rib injury, which would keep him out the following week. He was hoping it wasn't a replay of '79 with the injuries.

With Russ out, the team was buried by the Atlanta Falcons, 37-21, going completely flat in the second half after trailing just 28-21 at halftime. One writer point out the fact that the New England ground game suffered more than the passing game with Russ out. That's how essential his vicious blocking on the line is to the runners.

A week later Russ was back, catching three passes as the Pats whipped Seattle, 37-31, in another wild donnybrook. This time the Pats held up in the second half. The passing attack was really clicking. Stanley Morgan had become one of the most feared deep threats in the league, and the team often used a double tight end offense with Don Hasselbeck joining Russ in the lineup. Hasselback was 6-7 and a good receiver, though he didn't block nearly as well as Russ. After three weeks the club was tied with Miami at 2-1, trailing surprising Buffalo, still unbeaten at 3-0.

Then came a Monday night game with Denver. The Pats won it, 23-14, as Russ grabbed three more. Plus on two other occasions Russ was interfered with and the penalties paved the way for scores each time. Afterward, when asked if he had really been interfered with on one of the calls, Russ joked: "Oh, I thought my uncle was perfectly justified in making that call."

The next week the Jets fell, 21-11, and the Pats were sailing at 4-1, still a game behind the 5-0 Bills, but now ahead of both Miami and Baltimore at 3-2. They seemed to be dominating once again, especially offensively. There were still some worries about the defense, and of course, that strange letdown that seemed to grip the club several times every year, costing them dearly.

Not to worry, at least not now. For the following week they really put it together, destroying arch-rival Miami, 34-0, with a beautifully balanced attack. Russ had four catches for 51 yards and a score. He was healthy and contributing mightily each week. And with a Buffalo loss, the Pats were tied for first at 5-1.

A week later they were at it again. Facing the Colts, they trailed at halftime, 14-10. But in the second half they poured it on. Running back Don Calhoun scored on a 19-yard-run. Horace Ivory returned a kickoff 98-yards for a TD, John Smith kicked a pair of field goals and veteran Chuck Foreman bolted over from the one. It ended a 37-21 victory, putting the Pats at 6-1 and giving them sole possession of first place in the AFC East. As for Russ, he was being incredibly consistent, with three catches for 50 yards and his usual tough blocking.

"If there's a difference in this year's team and last year's it's attitude," said quarterback Grogan. "This year we have a winning attitude and some things are going right for us. We had to come up with some big plays to beat the Colts, and we did. We've been doing that all year."

But it always seems when the Patriots are the most optimistic they run into trouble. They traveled to Buffalo for a crucial game with the Bills and were beaten decisively, 31-13, dropping them back to 6-2 and into a first place tie. Russ got the Pats only touchdown, snaring a 26-yard pass from Grogan, as Buffalo running back Joe Cribbs gained 118 yards and the Patriot runners were limited to just 39.

The team had to bounce back fast, and seemed to have the perfect team with which to do it. They'd be meeting the New York Jets, a team that had won just two games all year. This was the kind of game the Patriots had been known to blow. But not this time. They got 17 points in the first quarter and took a 24-0 lead before cruising home, 34-21. Russ got the game's first touchdown making a nifty catch on a 33-yard pass from Grogan. He grabbed three more passes and was quietly putting together an outstanding season. Plus the club was back in first place at 7-2. It was hard to see how they could blow it this time.

Afterwards, a confident Ron Erhardt said, "I don't ever remember beating the Jets twice in one year when we had to. Any time you can double up a team in your division, you're on the road to the playoffs."

It was the next two weeks that hurt. First there was a battle royal with the powerful Houston Oilers. When the smoke cleared from that one, the Pats had lost a 38-34 decision, despite a brilliant day from Russ with five catches for 86 yards and two scores.

A week later it was another top team, the Los Angeles Rams. This one was a defensive battle. The Pats came from a 7-0 deficit to take a 14-7 lead at the half. But in the third period the Rams scored 10 points and neither team could get on the board in the fourth. So L.A. won it, 17-14, handing the

Pats their second loss in a row.

But you couldn't say same old Pats. In the Houston game they came from behind a 24-6 deficit and almost won it. With the Rams, it was a defensive struggle that could have gone the other way. Now the club was 7-4 and a game behind the Bills in the division race.

It all seemed back in place the next week when they whipped Baltimore, 47-21, coming up big on the ground. But after that they had one of those letdowns. They dropped a 21-17 decision to San Francisco, which intercepted six Grogan passes. Russ had four catches for 68 yards, but there was suddenly a feeling that the club was in trouble. They were 8-5, only a game behind Buffalo, but had lost three of their last five. Now they had to beat Miami the following Monday night. Well, they did their best. The game was a dogfight, deadlocked at 12-all at the end of regulation.

It went into sudden death, the whole season and playoffs possibly on the line. The Dolphins had the ball and moved downfield. They drove all the way to Patriot six-yard line. Then Ewe von Schamann came on and booted a 23-yard field goal to give the Dolphins a 16-13 victory.

The loss was a bitter one. Russ contributed just two catches, but one was a beautiful 38-yard TD reception. Still, he was as down as the rest of the team. They had gone from 7-2 to 8-6 and their chances of making the playoffs was dim. However, this time around the team did have an extremely difficult schedule and lost some close games to top teams. It wasn't that they had blown it as had been the case in the past.

And they did show their character in the final two games. First, they went up against division-leading Buffalo. A loss would definitely eliminate them. But they played extremely well and whipped the Bills soundly, 24-2. Russ had four catches in this one and snagged another six-pointer. The closing game would be against the New Orleans Saints. If the Patroits won, they could only get to the playoffs if Buffalo, Cleveland or San Diego lost their final games.

The Pats did their part. They whipped the Saints, 38-27. Russ finished up with two catches for 54 yards and a 39-yard scoring reception. Now he and the rest of his teammates held their breaths. Slowly, the bad news came in. Buffalo had beaten the 49ers, 18-13. Then Cleveland pulled it out with a last minute field goal to whip the Bengals, 27-24. Two down. But the Charger-Steeler game wasn't until Monday night.

As it turned out, the waiting was in vain. San Diego won the game handily, and at 10-6 for the year, the Patriots were nowhere, out of the playoffs for a second straight season, a season in which many predicted they'd be in the Super Bowl.

So they remain an enigma, a team loaded with talent, but one that can't seem to make that final breakthrough to bring them to the top of the heap, and earn them the respect accorded big winners. With the personnel they have, the Patriots may yet find the formula.

As for Russ Francis, the big guy had put together another fine year. Playing in 15 games he had a career high 41 catches for 664 yards and eight touchdowns. Those totals were also career highs. Russ's average of 16, 2 yards per catch was better than that of the other top tight ends in 1980. For instance, San Diego's Kellen Winslow, who caught 79 balls for over 1,000 yards and was touted so fast and quick as a tight end that he sometimes played wide receiver, averaged just 14.2 yards per catch. Mike Barber of Houston, another highly-touted tight end, had a 12.1 average. And the great Dave Casper also averaged 14.2.

So there's no doubt about Russ's ability. There are those who feel the Pats don't throw to him enough. Others say his blocking is so devastating they need him on the line throwing his weight around. And there are those who still feel he has a cavalier attitude toward his sport and hence to his team. But Russ Francis has ceased to worry about that kind of talk a long time ago. He knows what he can do, what he has done, and what he has meant to the Patriots. Not that he's perfect, but he's obviously close to or at the top of the list at his position.

Despite the problems the Patriots have encountered over the past five seasons or so, Russ still believes in his team, and looks forward to each season with optimism and enthusiasm. He still feels he can become a better player.

"With my blocking now," he said, toward the end of 1980, "I'm just trying to become a little quicker. As for my pass receiving, I think I've become more intense and have greater concentration. One of the things I like about tight end is that every pass pattern can be a new experience. I remember one game when I was complaining to an official about being mauled coming off the line of scrimmage. He told me since I was one of the premier tight ends in the game I should expect to draw a lot of attention.

"This is what keeps the job from becoming a bore. If you simply ran into the same defense every play, it wouldn't be a challenge. But I'm double and triple covered and I always have to keep adjusting, constantly."

That's Russ the player. But the other guy is still there, the one who looks at things in his own special way. Ask and he'll talk about that side, too.

"I've heard that business about not reaching my potential since high school. In the pros, it's been the same way. First I thought it was based on performance, but then I started to realize that people made those judgements based on something else. They seem to think that if you don't devote every single minute of your life to football, you can't be a complete player.

"If I flew a plane, or went sky diving, or drove a motorcycle, they kept on saying I was going to kill myself. If I went scuba diving, a shark was going to eat me. Well, let me tell you, if all I did was football, I'd be bored to death. Doing all the other things makes life an experience for me. I like to try new things and create new interest. And when it's time to play football, then I give it everything I have."

So that's Russ Francis, one of the originals, and one of the best tight ends to ever play the game. And when all is said and done, they'll probably paraphrase the words of that famous song to best describe him. Russ Francis was a man who did it his way.

John Jefferson

It was the opening day of the 1978 National Football League season, and the San Diego Chargers were playing the Seattle Seahawks at the Kingdome in Seattle. The Chargers were an up-and-coming team in the NFL and starting the season with high hopes. One reason was their quarterback, Dan Fouts, who was maturing into one of the best passers in the league.

Sure enough, early in the game Fouts had his club moving. When the drive reached the Seattle 29-yard line, the quarterback decided it was time to get his rookie wide receiver from Arizona State into the action. He called the play and broke the huddle.

At the snap, Fouts made that quick drop of his and looked for the rookie, who was heading for the end zone, two defenders around him. Fouts laid the ball up softly and as it came down in the end zone, the rookie leaped high and literally took the pigskin away from the defenders for a Charger touchdown.

The catch was John Jefferson's first ever in the National Football League, and fittingly, it went for a score. Later in the game, the man some sportswriters were already calling Lord Jeff or the Jefferson Airplane, caught another. It was only for six yards, but it went for another score, and again he caught it in heavy traffic, this time pulling it in with both hands over his head. San Diego won the game, 24–20, and John Jefferson repeated that he didn't care for the fancy nicknames. Just plain J.J. was fine with him.

But John Jefferson's nickname was not a real concern of the Chargers. They were more interested in what J.J. could do once the football was in the air. And they quickly found out what they had suspected and hoped for all along. He could get the ball, often in seemingly impossible situations, often in very heavy traffic, and often in an acrobatic, spectacular, and unbelievable manner. John "J.J." Jefferson was an electrifying pass receiver, the kind that comes along just a few times in each era.

J.J.'s auspicious debut proved no fluke. The only thing that has slowed him down since has been a few minor injuries. In the three years since he came into the league, J.J. has become an integral part of the most awesome passing attack in pro football history. Quarterback Fouts, throwing to J.J., Charlie Joiner, and Kellen Winslow, forms the heart of an offense that set a slew of passing records in the 1980 season. And they show no signs of slowing down.

As for J.J., he, too, has been a record-setter. Among other things, he is the first receiver in NFL history to gain more than 1,000 yards receiving in each of his first three seasons in the league. And the number of incredible, impossible, acrobatic—or however you want to describe them—catches is too large to count. He never gives up on a ball, never feels a pass is uncatchable, and never gives less than 100 percent, even if it means putting his body on the line.

Yet for all his success, John Jefferson hasn't really changed. He knew he wanted to be an NFL receiver for a long time, since early school days. Since then, he has worked long and hard, and without wavering, to achieve his goal. It influenced everything he did growing up, and even the college he decided to attend. And he made the gradual climb, from high school to college to pro without a ripple, or period of adjustment. He simply traveled his road with a quiet kind of confidence that never approached cockiness or arrogance.

When he joined the Chargers, J.J. found himself being compared to another great receiver of the past, Hall of Famer Lance Alworth. Even that didn't leave him in awe or with the feeling that he'd always have something to live up to.

"All the publicity I've gotten doesn't affect me," he said, "because I've heard the same thing all my life. Even in college I was being compared with the great receivers who were there before me."

Nor does the ferocious hitting and intimidation tactics of defensive backs upset him. J.J.'s secret has always been his amazing concentration, and the ability to shut everything out except getting the ball.

"No, I don't get upset about taking hard hits," he said. "It's part of the game. The defense has to try that kind of thing to get some respect. So I accept it, but I just refuse to let any of it bother me."

Is the picture becoming clearer? John Jefferson is an unusual young man. There is no pretense about him. He plays football because he loves it. Sure, the money doesn't hurt, but it isn't the primary concern. In fact, he even enjoys practicing, and always works as hard as anyone. He will report to training camp with the rookies if he feels he has to learn more. He wants to know the game plan and the plays with extreme precision, so he's always in exactly the place where Fouts and his teammates will expect him to be. As his coach, Don Coryell, puts it:

"J.J. is a fierce competitor and completely unselfish, and he really fires up during a game. His eyes get big. He loves to play, and he loves to practice. He's a real team guy."

John Larry Jefferson was born on February 3, 1956, one of four children born to James and Patty Jefferson of Dallas, Texas. Young J.J. was basically a happy youngster, and one who took to sports early, playing and excelling at all of them. His introduction to football came when he was in the fifth grade and attending the Sidney Johnson Elementary School in the Oak Cliff neighborhood.

"When J.J. was in the fifth or sixth grade he was already telling me he was going to play pro ball," his mother remembers. "Later, when I realized how serious he was about football, it scared me. But I never tried to stand in the way of any of my kids. While I didn't encourage his playing, I didn't discourage it, either."

She also remembers something else J.J. did during those early days when pro football was first on his mind.

"He already had a list of teams he wanted to play for," she recalls. "It included Minnesota, Los Angeles, Washington, and Dallas. I guess he was following them even then, though he didn't list San Diego as one of his favorites."

Robert Thomas, who would be J.J.'s coach when he reached Roosevelt High School in Dallas, remembers him as a young kid, and says he was always playing catch in his front yard, even after practices once he started playing with sandlot teams in the area. And his mother remembers him running pass routes by streetlight at night, and begging his friends to throw the football so he could catch it.

Yet he played other sports and was also outstanding at baseball and basketball, and later was a star on the track team as well. But there was one thing that disrupted an otherwise happy childhood. His parents split up, and his mother eventually remarried. So during most of his junior high and all of his high school years, he used his stepfather's name, and was known as John Washington.

When J.J. went to Oliver Wendell Holmes Junior High, he was becoming even more serious about football. Yet surprisingly, he played defensive end most of the time he was there, though he certainly didn't have the size or the bulk of a lineman. But playing out of position didn't deter him. He already gave 100 percent every time out and was winning awards for his play before he graduated.

Then it was on to Roosevelt where Robert Thomas became his coach. Thomas took one look at J.J.'s natural attributes, his speed, moves, and agility, and knew the kid was not a defensive end. Both coach and player were very happy about the switch to wide receiver, and as soon as Coach Thomas saw the way J.J. went out for passes and pulled them in, his eyes popped out. He knew immediately he had something special.

J.J. was a special kind of kid in other ways, as well. He always helped around the house and never balked when asked to do something for a family member or friend.

"He was always so great while he was growing up," his mother says. "I don't care what it was he was told to do, he'd always do it without hesitation. Even if it was something he didn't like, he'd just do it and I could never tell whether he was angry or not, because he never complained."

Plus J.J. always stayed busy doing positive things. Time was an important commodity and he didn't like wasting it, especially after he decided he wanted to be a professional athlete.

"I recall asking him once why he didn't go driving around the streets with his friends," his mother related, "and he said to me very quickly, 'I'm not going to start running the streets when I've got better things to do.' "

Once he went into action for Roosevelt High he really began making a name for himself. And he didn't take long to do it. It started in his sophomore year. Roosevelt was playing North Dallas and they were getting steamrolled. By halftime, North Dallas had a 32–0 lead that looked insurmountable. So at halftime, Coach Thomas decided to really see what J.J. was made of under pressure. He instructed his quarterback to put the ball in the air and try to get it to J.J. as much as possible.

The Roosevelt offense went to work, and suddenly John Jefferson was running wild. He was virtually unstoppable, getting wide open on numerous occasions, and making unreal catches in a crowd other times. When the smoke cleared, four of his receptions had gone for touchdowns and Roosevelt had a miraculous, 34–32, comeback victory.

After that, J.J. seemed to catch a slew of passes every week. No kind of defense could totally stop him, and if three or four players were put on him at once, it would free other members of the club. He was the focal point around which the entire team revolved.

By his senior year he was well on his way to setting all kinds of Texas schoolboy records for pass receiving, and the college recruiters were beginning to come around. It was said that during that year, the 1973 season, it was easy to find J.J.'s house. It was the one where the recruiters were always jostling each other for position.

"Sometimes it seemed there were lines in front of the house that stretched for a whole block," his mother remembers. "Some of them hung around until after midnight, waiting for a chance to try to sell J.J. on their schools."

J.J. himself was already thinking ahead, of course. Though also a track star at Roosevelt, having run the hundred in 9.6 and the 220 in 21.2, he knew early on that football was the way for him to go.

"Football just seemed to be more of a challenge for me," J.J. recalls. "It was the sport that gave me the most satisfaction and it also was the one that drew the largest crowds and loudest cheers, which gave me another kind of feeling. I loved it."

With the NFL his ultimate goal, J.J. was already studying pro receivers then.

"I watched all the receivers I could then," he says, "and I could just about tell you what all of them did best. One of my early heroes was Gene

Washington, who played for the Minnesota Vikings in the early 1970's. I remember really enjoying how he and Joe Kapp worked together one year. In fact, he's the reason I asked for number 84 when I got to college."

There were more memorable games during his senior year. He remembers a big one against archrival Carter High that season when Roosevelt had a 19–3 lead at the half and lost, 26–19.

"Something happened to us that day. I guess we got to celebrating too early and they came back to beat us. You really can't stop playing hard until that final gun sounds."

It wasn't all like that. In fact, that was the exception rather than the rule. Closer to the rule was the game against Woodrow Wilson High that year. J.J. grabbed eight passes in that one, good for the amazing total of 254 yards and three touchdowns. He could get them long or short, and if he got one short, his speed and agility made him a constant threat to turn it upfield long.

By the time the season ended, J.J. had really rewritten the high school record books. In three seasons he grabbed 161 passes for 3,997 yards and 41 touchdowns. That's an average of nearly 54 passes, 1,332 yards, and more than 13 touchdowns a year. And he topped it all off by being named Bluest of the Blue Chippers in a poll conducted by the Dallas *Times Herald*. That made him the top schoolboy football player in the state. The senior who finished second to J.J. was a fullback from Tyler named Earl Campbell. And everyone knows about Earl Campbell. That should just about spell out how good John Jefferson was at Roosevelt High.

"He was the most incredible player I ever coached," said Robert Thomas. "Yet he always stayed the same kid, with a cool, level head. He was a kid who never bragged, though he certainly had plenty to brag about, just the kind of guy you really like to have around. No, there's no doubt in my mind that he's the best I've ever seen or coached."

Now, of course, it was decision time. Where to go to continue his education and his football career. J.J. was being bombarded by recruiters and, as is always the case, by carloads of promises.

"It was quite an experience," J.J. recalls. "I was offered cars, clothes, apartments, you name it. They offered material things for my parents, scholarships for everybody in the family still in school. But my family was doing all right. We didn't need that kind of thing. In fact, they warned me against it."

Anyone who really knew J.J. would have realized this wasn't the right approach. For one thing, he was never really into material things, and hence not impressed by cars, clothes, and other things that bespoke of the flashy lifestyle. Secondly, his goal besides his education and a good environment in which to live and study, was to prepare himself for professional football. So those recruiters who called his home at two and three in the morning, hoping to get an extra word in, were probably wasn't their time. And when people from UCLA and Texas A&M showed up at 6:30 a.m. on the first day letters of intent could be signed, they, too, were basically wasting their time. J.J. was in the process of deciding in his own way.

For example, there was some heavy recruiting from the University of Texas, which was really J.J.'s hometown school, if there is such a thing. That's where Earl Campbell decided to go, but his reason for going there was part of J.J.'s reason for declining to become a Longhorn.

"Texas ran out of the wishbone," J.J. explained. "And to me that meant they weren't going to throw very much. It was tailor-made for Earl, as he proved, but I knew it wasn't what I wanted."

There were similar considerations when he looked at other schools. In fact, for a time it looked as if he would decide to go out to the coast and play at UCLA. Robert Thomas, who was helping J.J. make his choice, recalls just how close the kid came to picking the UClans.

"At one point," Thomas said "J.J. had pretty much made up his mind to go to UCLA. We even called them and told them J.J. was ready to sign. I think it was about 8:30 in the morning when we made the call. At about noon, one of the UCLA coaches came here to sign him, but we just couldn't find John. He was missing, and after a few hours, the guy gave up and left. That evening, J.J. came back and told me why he had ducked out. That same day we made the call, he received a pamphlet which said that Dick Vermeil, who was the coach then, was going to put in the Veer formation. So again, J.J. was faced with primarily a running formation that didn't feature too much passing. So he passed."

During this time, J.J. began to look more closely at Arizona State University. The Sun Devils played big time ball, but were probably not quite as well known as some of the perennial powerhouses such as Notre Dame, Texas, Ohio State, and USC. They also had a coach, Frank Kush, who had a reputation as one of the toughest in the country. But there were things there that J.J. liked.

"You never saw Arizona State games on television much," J.J. recalls. "But when you watched the pro games, it seems there were receivers all over the league who had played there. That seemed to speak well for their system, an offense that threw the ball."

A little more research showed that to be the case. Arizona State had spawned such pass-catching stars as Charley Taylor, Ben Hawkins, and J.D. Hill, as well as others who had gone on to the NFL. In fact, the Sun Devil offense was always pass oriented to the degree that after practice and dinner, the quarterbacks and receivers would often come back onto the field and work on their routes until 9 p.m.

"Coach Kush's teams can score from anywhere on the field," J.J. said. "And as far as the rugged practices and training camps are concerned, I've never minded hard work in my life. So that doesn't bother me at all."

So it was finally decided. J.J. would go to Tempe, Arizona, in the fall of 1974 to play for Arizona State. Thus ended another wild recruiting race, the kind that envelops so many young high school stars all around the country. But unlike some, J.J. took it all in stride, didn't allow himself to succumb to the pressure, took his time and made a clear, rational choice.

His final high school game was the Texas High School Coaches All-Star Game, for which the players had to spend some time practicing. J.J. even roomed with his old rival, Earl Campbell, before the game. The two became friends, but strangely enough, are looked upon in different ways today by football fans of the Lone Star State.

Campbell remained home, became a superstar at Texas, and has been an equally good professional with the Houston Oilers. So he's like an adopted son in Texas to this day. As for J.J., bear in mind that he went all through school, including his record-breaking years at Roosevelt, using the name John Washington. Then, John Washington decided to leave the state and go to college in Arizona.

When he arrived in Tempe, J.J. made a decision. He wanted to use his rightful father's name, and he entered Arizona State as John Jefferson, the name he has used ever since. From there, of course, he wound up playing pro ball in California. "I guess the people back home sort of lost track of me," he said. "They knew me as John Washington, and many of them probably didn't even know about my changing my name. So I've never been an overwhelming favorite back home."

At Arizona State, J.J. immediately impressed everyone connected with the football program. At 6–1, about 180 pounds then, he wasn't overly big, but he had all that natural ability, plus the kind of confidence that couldn't be shaken or intimidated. He adjusted to college ball without a ripple and became a Sun Devil starter as a freshman, not an easy accomplishment with a taskmaster coach such as Frank Kush.

It was almost amazing the way he took everything new in stride. His quiet confidence never left, no matter how hard training camp at Tortozona (the name given Kush's infamous summer practice camp), no matter how hard the coaches pushed him. He worked hard to learn the system and get himself in top shape. Then he was ready.

"When you take a new step, like high school to college, at first you think to yourself 'Hey, these players are great,' " J.J. explained. "But in a short time you find out they're just regular players, and you know you can step right in."

Coming from someone else, that would sound like cockiness, bragging. But from J.J., it was simply the truth, the way he saw things and the way he felt. He would say it, but he would also go out and do it. For example, he never let a defensive back intimidate him. Running pass routes across the middle, perhaps the easiest way for a receiver to be injured, J.J. would just concentrate on getting the ball. If he was hit hard, so be it. He'd bounce up and run his next pattern across the middle just a little bit harder. By the time the game was over, it was the defensive back who was intimidated, if by nothing else by the simple fact that he couldn't stop John Jefferson no matter what he tried to do.

So J.J. stepped in and quickly became the Sun Devils most reliable and most spectacular receiver as a freshman. It wasn't long into the season before the coaches and the rest of the team counted on him in the clutch. Again, he took it in stride.

"People have been counting on me all my life. I knew they were counting on me as a freshman and I think I played pretty well."

Yes, he did. The Sun Devils had a young team in 1974 and managed just a 7–5 record, but John showed he was a force with 30 catches for 423 yards and one touchdown. When you think that there was a time not so many years ago when freshmen couldn't play varsity ball because it was thought they weren't mature enough, physically or mentally, J.J. had quite a season.

The following year, he really made his presence felt. This time the Sun Devils were a tough club. The youngsters had matured, and a good crop of seniors were ready for a last hurrah. The team began winning and J.J. was catching more balls

than ever. Then came the big game with tradition
rival Arizona. This was the one everybody wanted
to win. Besides thoughts of an unbeaten season,
State pride was at stakes, the proverbial bragging
rights.

It was the final regular-season game, so each
club was letting out all the stops. Arizona got the
better of it, and had a 14–3 lead with time running
out in the first half. The Sun Devils were driving
and moved deep into Arizona territory. With just
30 seconds remaining, quarterback Dennis Sproul
dropped back to pass, looking for J.J.

The wide receiver was streaking into the end
zone when Sproul fired the ball, hard and on a line.
At the last second, J.J. dived, his body flat-out in
mid-air, his hands extended as far as they could go.
Still, it looked to everyone as if the ball was past
him and incomplete. But when J.J. hit the ground,
the ball was in his hands! No one could believe he
had caught it. Everyone watching would swear the
pass was already beyond his reach.

Even today, that reception is still known simply
as "The Catch" in Sun Devil territory. It brought
the Sun Devils back in the game, gave them the
boost they needed. In the second half they dominated, J.J. grabbing another touchdown aerial, and
they won it, 24–21, to finish the regular season unbeaten.

It was a great year for J.J. He had 44 catches for
808 yards and five scores. He also averaged 18.4
yards per catch and his name began appearing on
some All-America teams. That's not easy at Arizona State. Players there don't usually get the recognition accorded stars at the more prestigious football schools.

There was still one more game to play. It wasn't

the Orange Bowl or Cotton Bowl, where other unbeaten teams might appear. The Sun Devils were
going to the Fiesta Bowl, but would be meeting a
very good Nebraska team. The Cornhuskers led
most of the way, though Arizona State hung tough.

Finally, in the fourth period, the Sun Devils
made a final drive. With the game on the line,
quarterback Sproul looked for J.J. and the fleet
wide receiver made another brilliant catch in the
end zone to give his team a 17–14 victory, and a
perfect, 12–0, season.

By 1976, J.J. was a seasoned veteran, and one of
the leaders of the Sun Devil team. Even Frank
Kush, a coach who is not easy to impress and not
one to throw the praise around with abandon,
began talking about his junior wide receiver whenever he had the chance.

"John leads by example," the coach said.
"There's no harder worker on the practice field.
He's not a hollar guy, but when the other players
see J.J. busting his butt in practice and in the
games, they suck it up and go with him."

But practice was always important to J.J. That
was the time he could work on his patterns, his
moves, his quickness, and getting the execution
down perfectly, so when the game rolled around,
he was totally prepared.

"We work real hard," he said. "We practice until 9 p.m. some nights, then shower, go home,
study, and go to bed. There's not much time for
anything else. But we have some unbelievable passing drills. Sometimes we even work without a ball.
The receivers run patterns against time, a buzzer
letting us know when the ball would be released.
All this helps us with execution, and its really
helped me immensely."

One thing J.J. was asked about constantly were his spectacular catches, his full length dives, and the self-inflicted beatings they seemed to produce.

"I know people seem to think some of my catches are spectacular," he said, "but to me it's just everyday work. It comes naturally and, no, I don't get that beat up from hitting the ground. Maybe if we played on artificial turf regularly it would, but fortunately in Arizona we have natural grass."

To some, this would again appear to be a cocky athlete, claiming the spectacular was just routine. But amazingly enough, with J.J., it was. He had been doing it all his football life and, indeed, it did come naturally.

The Sun Devils were not the same powerful team they had been in 1975. They had a tough schedule and had lost some top players through graduation. It was going to be a battle just to finish at .500. It didn't help when J.J. got banged up in the early going and was slowed for a couple of weeks. But when he got untracked, he was better than ever, despite a lesser cast of characters around him. Soon, the big games started to come.

In a 14–0 losing effort against Cincinnati, J.J. still managed eight catches for 105 yards. And when the Sun Devils went up against Brigham Young, their defense broke down completely. They lost the game, 43–21, yet J.J. still couldn't be stopped. He caught seven balls for 109 yards and Sun Devil receiver coach Richard Mann couldn't say enough about him.

"If J.J. can touch the ball, he'll catch it," Mann claimed. "And you'd be surprised at some of the footballs he can touch. That's what separates him from other receivers. He'll make the impossible grab and it always seems to come just when you need it the most."

Once again, J.J. saved his best game for last, the season-ending clash with Arizona. Going in, the Sun Devils had just a 3–7 record, making it a terribly disappointing season, especially following the unbeaten campaign of a year earlier. But a win over Arizona would at least be somewhat of a redemption. Knowing that, J.J. went to work.

It seemed whenever the Sun Devils needed a first down or a big play, J.J. was open. And if he wasn't open, he'd still emerge from the crash of bodies with the football. Early in the game when the Sun Devils trailed, he made a nifty 38-yard reception that set up the go-ahead score. After that, he led the team to a big, 27–10 victory with eight catches for 121 yards. It enabled him to end his junior year with 48 receptions for 681 yards and five more touchdowns. He seemed to be getting better and better, and by now the pro scouts were coming to Tempe to look at this lightning bolt from Texas.

One of those who saw him was Tank Younger, a former NFL running back and currently Assistant General Manager of the San Diego Padres. Younger was so impressed that he returned again during J.J.'s senior year. Then he had this assessment.

"I think John can be as good as anyone coming into the NFL the past ten years. When I saw him as a junior I knew right away he had the makings of a fine receiver. Then when I came back his senior year, I felt he was more ready to play in the NFL than any wide receiver I had ever seen. It was very obvious that he already had all the talents a great wide receiver had to have."

John's senior year of 1977 was, in effect, more of

the same, only he was better. He worked as hard at training camp and in practices as he had as a freshman. And once the season started he was all over the field. His play led the usually reticent Frank Kush to rave some more.

"J.J. is simply the best receiver I've ever coached. He's a tough kid who never once complained about working hard or about the bumps and bruises he received game after game. I just don't think I'll ever see another John Jefferson in my lifetime and to tell the truth, I don't think he's as good as he's gonna be yet."

Kush wasn't the only one. After J.J. had another field day in a 33–31 victory over Oregon State, Beaver coach Craig Fertig found it hard to believe what he had just seen.

"Nothing we did stopped or even slowed him," said Fertig. "As far as I'm concerned, there's nobody in the National Football League who could single cover John Jefferson right now."

Other coaches were just as enthusiastic. A prime example was Terry Donahue of UCLA, whose team didn't even play the Sun Devils that year, but who watched J.J. in other games. Said Donahue:

"I've never seen a more aggressive receiver than John Jefferson. He catches the ball anywhere and it's impossible for a defensive back to intimidate him. If there's a better receiver anywhere, I haven't seen him yet."

College coaches usually don't go quite this far in praise of a player, especially one who isn't on their own team. To see J.J. in action was to become a believer. The kid had it, all right. He finished his college career playing with a good 9–3, Sun Devil team, and this time he couldn't be ignored nationally.

As a senior he grabbed 53 passes for 912 yards, eight scores, and an average of 17.2 yards per catch. He even managed a touchdown rushing on an end around. His receiving stats had improved with each season and he finished his career with 175 catches for 2,824 yards and 19 touchdowns. And he wound up averaging 16.1 yards per catch for his career.

His outstanding efforts as a senior finally earned him national recognition. He was a first team All-American on many of the major polls and was an obvious projected first-round choice of an NFL team.

By this time, of course, J.J. was well aware that he'd be picked high. He knew he couldn't dictate where he would play, but he thought he might be able to influence the selection. So he went about it in the same quiet, rational way he had decided on a college four years earlier.

First of all, he knew he wasn't the only outstanding wide receiver coming out of college in 1978. Two other potential great ones were James Lofton of Stanford and Wes Chandler of Florida. The Green Bay Packers had the third pick in the 1978 draft and the Pack wanted a wide receiver. Club officials contacted J.J. before the draft and told him they were interested.

"I went up to Green Bay and talked with Bart Starr (the Packer coach) personally," J.J. said. "I told him I had lived in a warm climate all my life and knew I wouldn't be happy there. I just didn't want to live in the cold. I guess they didn't want someone who wouldn't be happy, so they passed."

New Orleans was another team drafting early who were looking for a wide receiver. There was no weather problem in Louisiana, but rather, let us say, an artistic problem. The Saints wanted a receiver who could double as a punt and kickoff returner. Though a complete team player, J.J. felt taking on this kind of double duty would not benefit either himself or the club.

"I'd never been a runback man before and I just didn't want to start," he said, flat out. "I think it would increase the possibility of injury, cut my effectiveness as a receiver, and ultimately shorten my career. I made these feelings known to the Saints."

Meanwhile, the San Diego Chargers were also looking quite seriously at J.J. Like most other teams, if they had their choice of any player in the draft, they probably would have picked Earl Campbell. J.J.'s old Texas buddy from high school years had become a Heisman Trophy-winning running back at Texas and the kind of player who might turn a franchise around. But there was no way he'd still be available when the Chargers picked. They had the 14th choice in the first round.

Charger coach Tommy Prothro had six names on his list of the best of the eligible collegians. J.J. was on the list, as was Campbell, Chandler, Lofton, as well as offensive linemen Chris Ward and Gordon King.

On the day of the draft, Prothro and his staff sat back and waited, holding their breaths. Houston picked first and grabbed Campbell, as expected. New Orleans, picking third, took Wes Chandler, and Green Bay, picking sixth, tabbed Lofton. Apparently, J.J.'s telling them he wouldn't be pleased playing for them had influenced their decision. By the tenth pick all of Prothro's six standouts had been taken . . . except J.J. But there were three more selections before San Diego's turn came, and as Prothro said:

"We sweated it out. We were really concerned."

But when it came time to choose, the man was still available and the announcement came quickly.

THE SAN DIEGO CHARGERS PICK JOHN JEFFERSON, WIDE RECEIVER, ARIZONA STATE!

It was done, and J.J. couldn't have been happier. "I rejoiced when the Chargers picked me. I wanted to play in the sunshine. In fact, believe it or not I was wearing a Charger T-shirt when I found out about the selection. I had gotten it when I was in San Diego with the Kodak All-American team in the fall."

The Chargers were another of the original American Football League teams, organized when the AFL began play in 1960. Actually, the franchise began play in Los Angeles and moved to San Diego the following season. The team was one of the early powers in the AFL, winning the Western Division title that very first year the AFL was in operation.

They repeated as division winners the following season, then in 1963 trounced the then Boston Patriots, 51–10, to win the AFL championship. They were in the title game again the next two years, losing to Buffalo each time, but over their first six seasons in the AFL the Chargers compiled an impressive, 54–28–4 mark.

There were some great individual stars on those early Charger teams, players like quarterback John Hadl, running backs Paul Lowe and Keith Lincoln, offensive tackle Ron Mix, and defensive linemen Ernie Ladd and Earl Faison. And then there was perhaps the best of them all, wide receiver Lance Alworth, the man they called "Bambi," an aerial acrobat who electrified fans for a decade and would become the first American Football League player elected to the Pro Football Hall of Fame. He was the player that J.J. would be compared with so often after he joined the Chargers.

The team continued to play winning football through 1969, but with the AFL-NFL merger in 1970, the franchise began to crumble. There were to be seven losing seasons in a row, with some real downers among them, such as a 2–11–1 mark in 1973 and a 2–12 slate in '75. Then the team seemed to be coming on, finishing with a 6–8 mark in '76 and a final .500 record, 7–7, in 1977. So, naturally, there were high hopes for '78, the year that J.J. was drafted and would be joining the team.

Veteran football man Sid Gillman was the club's first coach, and he ran the club for a decade through all its glory years. Three others had come and gone from 1970 until the appointment of Tommy Prothro in 1974. It was hoped that he was the man to restore the franchise to its former glory. And the results in '76 and '77 seemed to show he was on the right track.

There were already some fine football players on the Charger roster by 1978. It started with the quarterback, Dan Fouts, a passer of great potential. But Fouts had sat out a good deal of 1977 with contract problems. He returned for the final games and looked better than ever. He seemed ready to take his place among the premier passers in the NFL.

There was also a great draft in 1975. The team picked up defensive tackles Gary Johnson and Louie Kelcher, defensive backs Mike Williams and Mike Fuller, and defensive end Fred Dean. All would become starters and really make their presence known about the time J.J. joined the team.

There were some other good draft picks the next two years, and also the acquisition of some established veterans to give the team balance and stability. Players like defensive end Leroy Jones, offensive guard Ed White, running back Lydell Mitchell, and wide receiver Charlie Joiner came to the team in this manner. So many experts were picking the Chargers to get into the AFC Western Division race in 1978.

After the draft, J.J. began negotiating his first pro contract with the Chargers. He didn't feel it would be a problem, but it still wasn't settled when the team held a mini-camp in early May for rookies and first year players, as well as some veterans. Ordinarily, unsigned players will not attend these camps. Their agents usually advise against it, telling them they're still not really part of the team, and any kind of freak injury would greatly hamper their bargaining position.

Well, John Jefferson not only showed up, he was the star attraction. In an early passing drill he sprinted down the sideline, made a leaping one-handed catch, and somersaulted over, coming to a stop just a yard or two from the parking lot gate as everyone held their breaths. When someone told J.J. he could have racked himself up, he just laughed.

"That's just the way I am," he said. "I try to get every pass any way I can."

J.J. played that way for the length of the camp. He just snared everything thrown his way, leaping, diving, catching them high and low. Even the coaching staff, which had rated him above Chandler and Lofton in the draft, couldn't believe how good he looked. Nor could they or the veterans believe his poise and confidence. As one San

Diego writer, who had covered the team for a number of years, put it:

"Right away you could see there was something different about him. Something about the way he walked and carried himself. Something about the quiet confidence he seemed to exude. John Jefferson looked less like a rookie than any first-year player in Charger history.

"The kid wasn't wide-eyed, he wasn't nervous. He didn't jump when a coach called out his name. He never once seemed lost or bewildered. After 10 minutes on the Charger practice field, John Jefferson looked as if he had been there ten years."

Quarterback Fouts, just one of the players who would benefit directly because of J.J.'s presence, couldn't believe his new young receiver.

"He amazes me already," said Fouts. "I'll throw a ball poorly and say to myself, 'Shoot, you missed that one.' Then I'll look up and see that J.J.'s caught it. I've never seen anybody go to the ball the way he does. He makes great catches every practice session."

And veteran Charlie Joiner, who would be playing opposite J.J. at wideout, also commented on what the youngster would mean to the team's passing game.

"He's going to help us in so many ways," Joiner said. "Sooner or later they'll have to start double-teaming him, and that's when we'll be in business."

As much as he impressed in the mini-camp, J.J. talked as if the best was yet to come.

"I've got to get to know the system," he said. "Once I pick up the plays, I'll be more relaxed, and I'm pretty sure my performance will pick up. I do feel I will produce because I have confidence in myself and my ability."

It didn't take long for contract negotiations to end on a positive note. By early June, J.J. had signed. Terms were not disclosed, but it was believed that John signed a series of four, one-year contracts worth about $400,000. At any rate, J.J. was happy. Now he could relax and really go to work.

When he reported to the Chargers' training camp in July, he continued to impress everyone, and the comparisons with Lance Alworth began once again. The Chargers really hadn't had a gamebreaking receiver since. Coach Prothro couldn't have been happier.

"I have never seen a rookie receiver who looks as good as J.J.," the coach said. "He's got intelligence, great hands, very good speed and good instincts as a receiver. In fact, his instincts about getting open are as good as most receivers who have been in the league five or six years."

The Charger receiver coach that year was Ray Perkins, now head coach with the Giants. He, too, couldn't say enough about the youngster out of Arizona State.

"Right now," said Perkins, "I don't think there is another wide receiver in the entire NFL who goes for the ball like J.J. He can be a fine player because he's an intense guy, very intelligent, and has good discipline."

Remember, all this praise was being bantered about after just a short time in training camp. The preseason games hadn't even begun. So J.J. was hearing from everyone how great he was supposed to be, and how he was going to be another Lance Alworth. Pressure? Perhaps, but J.J. didn't seem to be letting it bother him.

"I remember seeing Lance Alworth when I was a

kid," J.J. said. "He was always getting open, had good hands and great concentration. I still have a lot to learn before I can be like him."

Once the preseason games began, J.J. proved that everything that had come before, all the praise, all the promise, was no fluke. He was all over the field, catching passes against experienced, veteran defensive backs. And each game, it seemed, he'd make a couple of his patented circus grabs.

In the third exhibition against the New York Jets, the entire Charger team was flat, and the Jets won easily, 23–10. The only man they couldn't contain was J.J. Jefferson. He ran wild, grabbing eight Fouts aerials for 134 yards and was virtually unstoppable. After three games, he had 17 grabs for 288 yards and was the leading receiver in the entire AFC during the preseason. And his attitude was to take it all in stride.

"The whole thing is really no different here than it was at Arizona State," he said. "In some cases it's been easier. Physically, training camp wasn't as rough as the ones at ASU, I can tell you that. As for the games, I can honestly say I wasn't trying that hard in preseason, not always going all out. When the regular season starts it'll be time to really go to work."

J.J. was also pleased that the NFL had passed new rules prohibiting defensive backs from bumping the receivers while they ran their patterns. That would eliminate the old bump-and-run defense.

"Yeah, that's to my advantage," J.J. said. "I've always had to rely on my quickness and moves, and I've got all the moves. All I need is a little room to operate. The new rules give me the room."

The second game of the preseason that year had been against the Los Angeles Rams, one of the

tougher defensive teams in the league, and it gave
J.J. a chance to see the kind of intimidation that
veterans might try. He responded beautifully.

"On the first play from scrimmage, their cornerback, Pat Thomas, came up and was going to
take a little shot at me," he said. "But he changed
his mind when I quickly responded. I hit him in the
Adams' apple with my wrist, and I'm sure it hurt
him. It was the last time he tried something like
that all night.

"What it amounts to is that I refuse to be intimidated. I ran across the middle all through college and they were never able to take me off my
game."

In the final preseason contest against the Giants,
J.J. didn't play much, just saw some duty on special teams. So, obviously, the Chargers felt he was
ready. They had seen he had the ability to handle
himself in all kinds of situations, and he usually
came away with the ball. His boyish, usually smiling face also masked a special kind of toughness
that all the great ones seem to have.

There was one tragic incident that marred the
entire preseason for all the NFL teams and players.
New England wide receiver Darryl Stingley was injured severely when he was hit while trying to catch
a ball thrown over the middle. Stingley sustained a
broken neck and it was doubtful whether he would
ever walk again.

Though he was the victim of a hard hit, it was a
clean one, and it probably made all the league's
wide receivers think about it more than anyone
else.

"Sure, it makes you think," J.J. said, when asked
about the incident. "But you can't think about it
too long if you want to do your job. You just can't

allow yourself to become timid in this game. You hate to see something like that happen, but it was a legal hit and these things will just happen sometime. As a receiver, you simply can't let anything take you off your game, even something as tragic as that."

But, come rain, snow, sleet, hail, the season must open. And the Chargers were at Seattle to begin what they hoped would be a banner year, one culminating in their first playoff appearance since 1965. And it was a fine debut, for both the team and John J.J. Jefferson. His first catch was the 29-yarder for the score, and his third, a six-yarder for six points. In between there was a 10-yard grab and the Chargers won the game, 24–20.

It seemed to be a promise of things to come, but it wasn't. The next week the club lost a close, 21–20, verdict to powerful Oakland, and the following week they were beaten by Denver, 27–14. What made the losses even tougher to take was the fact that these were considered the two best teams in the division, and if the Chargers were to make a run at it, they would have to beat the contenders.

Green Bay was up next, and some reporters tried to make a big deal about the meeting of the two first-round draftees, J.J. and James Lofton, who was playing for the Packers. J.J. played well in both losses, though slightly slowed by a groin pull. He had three TD catches, but felt he should be catching more passes. Lofton had already put together one big game, catching for three scores against New Orleans. But J.J. didn't go for the comparison stuff.

"I approach the game as win and lose," he said. "Whatever he does, he does; whatever I do, I do."

Unfortunately, for the Chargers and for J.J.,

they were never really in the game. Quarterback Fouts was playing with a sore thumb, J.J. had the slight groin pull, running back Lydell Mitchell was being eased into the lineup following off-season knee surgery. The team just wasn't competitive and were beaten handily by a Packer team that was mediocre at best. The final was 24–3, and the season of bright promise seemed ready to go down the tubes after four games. The club was 1–3 and struggling.

Several days after the Packer loss the team received the news that there would be a coaching change. Prothro had been under tremendous pressure to produce and with the dismal start, he resigned. Part of the reason also might have been the long-standing rumor that Charger owner Gene Klein wanted another coach. He was Don Coryell, who had coached the St. Louis Cardinals quite successfully for a number of years. When Coryell left the Cards the year before, it became an open secret that the Chargers wanted him. He was from the San Diego area and prior to going to the Cards, had a long and very successful coaching career at San Diego State.

Sure enough, immediately after Prothro resigned, Coryell was hired to replace him. No matter how they felt about Prothro, Croyell's coming was not exactly bad news for J.J., Fouts, Joiner, and the rest of the offense. For if one knew nothing else about Don Coryell, there was one bit of common knowledge. He was an offensive-minded coach and he loved to throw the football.

Though he still didn't have time to fully institute his system when the club went up against New England the following week, Coach Coryell instructed Fouts and his receivers to go to work. The result was a wide-open game between two high-powered offenses. It was J.J.'s kind of game.

With just 29 seconds left in the half, the rookie receiver streaked into the end zone and grabbed a 21-yard TD toss from Fouts, beating the speedy Raymond Clayborn. Then in the third quarter it happened again, J.J. beating Clayborn and scoring from 41 yards out. The only problem was the Charger defense wasn't quite equal to the task and San Diego lost again, 28–23. But many of the Chargers sensed a difference in the team.

"We went into the Green Bay game as two touchdown favorites and played flat," J.J. said. "But we were up for New England and well prepared. And we came close."

"I'm proud of the ballclub," Coryell said. "They had to come from behind to beat us and that's because they had the ball last. But we're coming of age as a team, wait and see."

After five games, J.J. had 13 receptions for 221 yards and five scores. He was already tied for the league lead in touchdown catches, but he wasn't satisfied with the stats he had compiled. He wanted to do better.

"To tell the truth, I thought I'd have more receptions," he said. "A couple of nagging injuries have held me back a bit, but I should start picking up more very soon. As for the TD's, they're nice, but making touchdowns is like making any other catch, just being in the right spot at the right time. I'd rather have more receptions and leave the touchdowns to the running backs."

Yet even with his desire to do better, J.J. said the transition from college to pro hadn't been difficult.

"I haven't really had any problems," J.J. said. "It's really not that much different to me. Basically, we're doing the same things we did at Arizona State. So the same principles apply. You have to have concentration and keep your mind on the game. Because I'm young and a rookie, they still try to take my mind off the game. But as I've said before, I just don't think that's possible."

Don Coryell was also very high on the rookie receiver and undoubtedly saw the possibilities of an incredible passing attack built around Fouts and Jefferson.

"J.J. just has great ability and is extremely intelligent," said the new coach. "Show him what to do once and he does it correctly. Some guys you can show 25 times and they still blow it. J.J. also has great balance and body control, and a great pair of hands.

"I'd say that's a pretty good combination, smarts and tremendous desire, the ambition to be great, and all the tools to make it happen."

The following week the Chargers put it all together, with a big, 23–0, win over Denver. J.J. played well and contributed, though he still didn't have that real big game. But the groin pull was healed and he expected to break loose any week. Of course, there's still one thing in sports that all the ability in the world can't overcome—an injury. Against Miami the next week J.J. took a finger in the eye and had to leave the game. The retina of the eye had been scraped, a potentially dangerous injury, especially if it happens a second time.

"That's true," J.J. said. "The doctor told me if it happened again, I could go blind in the eye."

So he sat out two weeks. The club had lost the Miami game, 28–21, then were beaten by a weak Detroit team, 31–14. The following week they bounced back for a big, upset win over Oakland, as

Fouts hit tight end Greg McCrary for a TD with 52 seconds left. The final of that game was 27–23, but the club had just a 3–6 record and seemed all but out of the playoff picture for another year.

The next game was against Cincinnati, and J.J. was due back. He was ready, but with a new piece of equipment—a pair of goggles to protect his eyes. They were similar to the ones worn by Kareem Abdul-Jabbar on the basketball court, and for the same reason. There was no way J.J. wanted the eye injury to recur.

Against Cincinnati, J.J. was getting open and Fouts began hitting him. The combo clicked all afternoon and the Chargers took a 22–13 victory, with J.J. nailing six passes for 97 yards. He looked as if he was really ready to roll. The next week he proved it.

The Chargers were up against another old AFL rival, the Kansas City Chiefs, and it was a tooth and nail struggle all the way. For four periods the two teams battled, and wound up in a 23–23 tie. J.J. was having another big day, beating the defensive backs repeatedly and once again making his circus-type catches.

Yet the game went into sudden death overtime. For nearly fifteen minutes more the two teams battled, neither one able to put the finishing points on the board. With time running out in the OT period, the Chargers began driving. If they didn't make it here, the game would end a tie. It had been raining and the field was slick and wet, but the Chargers kept moving. Finally they reached the K.C. 14-yard line with just 29 seconds left.

But could they get another play off in time? Fouts got them to the line and with time running out lofted one into the end zone. There was J.J., keeping his feet as the defender fell down, making the catch for the winning score.

"When I was at the line," J.J. said, afterward, "I took a glance at the clock and knew it was tight. Dan threw the ball to the wettest part of the field. I saw their cornerback, Tim Collier slip and go down, then saw the ball coming. When I caught it I looked around to see if there were any flags, then I started jumping up and down because I knew we had won."

The winning catch capped J.J. best game as a pro. He had grabbed seven balls for 130 yards and two scores. The win was the club's third in a row and brought their record to 5–6. And despite missing two games and part of another, J.J. now had 32 catches for 513 yards and seven scores. His stats were the best of any rookie receiver in the league.

A week later he was the hero again. The Chargers were battling the Minnesota Vikings in the snow and cold of Metropolitan Stadium, the kind of weather J.J. liked to avoid. In the third period, with the Chargers trailing, 7–6, Fouts drove his club to the 10. Then, at the line of scrimmage, he called an audible, changed the play, but J.J. didn't hear it because of the crowd noise.

"I lost my footing when I dropped back," quarterback Fouts said, "and when I regained it and looked for J.J., he wasn't where he should have been. I knew he hadn't heard the audible. Then I spotted him over the middle in traffic, but I also saw a hole."

Fouts rifled the ball and J.J. grabbed it with his quick hands between two defenders and tumbled into the end zone with the TD that proved the difference in a 13–7 final. The team was suddenly 6–6 after four straight wins and for the first time there was talk of the playoffs.

"I ran the play called in the huddle," said J.J. "The audible was for an out pattern, but I ran over the middle. I guess it ended up OK. Hey, I've got a lot more up my sleeve. Whatever it's going to take, I'm willing to do. We all are. That's why we're going to the playoffs."

Everyone was very optimistic, riding a four-game high, and now that the club was learning Coryell's system, it seemed as if the team was beginning to play to its true potential. Then a strange thing happened, one of those inexplicable results that so often occur in professional sports. In spite of the good feeling and renewed confidence, the team traveled to Kansas City and came out completely flat. They were shut out by a team they had beaten in overtime just two weeks earlier, 23–0.

The following week the team hosted the always-rugged Chicago Bears. With just three games left, this was a big one. The Chargers were at 6–7 and wanted at least a .500 season. That would be quite an accomplishment after the 2–6 first half. In addition, the Bears game was a nationally televised Monday night contest. There would be a huge audience.

What those tuning in saw was John Jefferson at the top of his game. The Bears just couldn't stop him. J.J. and Fouts knew it and they hooked up time and again for long gains. When the game ended, the Chargers had an impressive, 40–7, victory, and J.J. had the best game of any Charger receiver in the past six years.

He had grabbed seven Fouts aerials for 155 big yards and a touchdown. It was a very happy J.J. after the game.

"We had a national crowd and really wanted to

do it," he said. "We were really emotional tonight and a lot of the credit for that has to go to Coach Coryell. He gives pregame speeches and really gets excited, which helps us a lot. And it doesn't hurt that we throw a lot more passes, either.

"We've had some bad breaks this year, but mainly, we've messed up against the teams we should have beaten, the weaker teams like Green Bay, Detroit, and Kansas City. Now we've got to win our final two games and finish at 9–7. Then we can come to camp next year with that momentum. Those things to carry over."

While J.J. was meeting increasing success on the field, he was living a rather quiet lifestyle off it. He shared an apartment with another rookie, Ricky Anderson. Neither owned a car or went in for other material things such as flashy clothes and jewelry. And they didn't spend a lot of time out on the town.

"No, I don't get out much," J.J. said, "and people don't know how to find me. I'm isolated, and I kind of like that. At this stage, people want to get into you for what you have."

J.J. also had a rather conservative and careful approach to handling his money. Plus he was already looking to a time when he wouldn't be playing ball anymore.

"I think I got an excellent contract," he said. "I'm not greedy, and money doesn't really excite me. But if you're going to take that beating out there, no use in being short-changed. And if you're a star player, there's no sense in making less money than someone on the bench. These are the things I keep in mind."

J.J. had taken some of his money and bought his family a new home. He also invested some of it in real estate, then banked the rest to see what would happen with his investments. He wasn't about to put all the eggs in one basket.

"If I utilize my money right I don't think I'll ever have to get an office job," he said. "And I should be able to use the football part of my life to better the part that comes after. Two areas I hope to explore when the time comes are broadcasting and youth work."

So J.J. seemed to be in full control of his life as the final games of his rookie season approached. First the Chargers whipped Seattle again, 37–10, as J.J. grabbed four tosses for 66 yards. Now the club had to go against playoff-bound Houston in the finale. And the Oilers were led by rookie Earl Campbell, who was leading the NFL in rushing his freshman year.

But J.J. wasn't doing so badly either. He already had caught 50 passes 852 yards. It was conceivable that he could reach 1,000 yards with a big game against the Oilers. And it was being played in the Astrodome, so he'd be performing in his home state of Texas.

The Oilers were a solid team. Besides the Campbell-led offense, they had a hard-hitting, rock-ribbed defense, but on this particular Sunday, a flotilla of battleships would have had trouble stopping the San Diego offense and John J.J. Jefferson. The Chargers rolled to an easy, 45–24, victory, and J.J. grabbed six passes for 149 yards and two more touchdowns. He once again showed his toughness by finishing the game despite a slight shoulder separation suffered in the second period.

When the game ended, quarterback Fouts, who had thrown for 369 yards couldn't stop talking about J.J.

"He's an all-Pro, without question," the QB said. "I just can't say enough about him. I've never seen anybody, anywhere who is better."

Again J.J. made one of those statements that could be taken for cockiness or bragging, but with him it's just the words of a confident athlete who knows his own abilities very thoroughly.

"I'm just doing something I did in high school at Roosevelt, something I did in college at Arizona State. It's really no big deal."

But it was a big deal. J.J. had completed his rookie season with 56 catches for 1,001 yards and 13 touchdowns. His TD mark tied a rookie record set 26 years earlier by Bill Howton of Green Bay. And in the final three games of the season, when the Chargers outscored their opponents, 122–41, J.J. had 17 catches for 370 yards. He was playing better than he had all season. And he already knew what that would mean the next year.

"I'll probably get a lot of double coverage next year," he said. "So in order to get me open we're going to have to pick 'em apart on the other side and to use our backs. It'll probably be difficult for me to match my rookie stats, though if I stay healthy it's possible. But defenses today are so complicated that I don't think you'll be able to catch 70 or 80 passes a year any more the way guys like Lance Alworth did."

The only slight downer in the final game was the fact that J.J.'s touchdown record was not announced over the public address system at the Astrodome. He felt he should have had that recognition in his home state. But he also knew that people remembered him as John Washington, and some of his identity had been lost. Plus there was another fact he acknowledged.

"This is Houston and it's Earl Campbell country," he said. "They don't want anybody to know another rookie has set a record."

Campbell was something else. He had set a rookie mark by leading the NFL with 1,450 yards rushing. So he would be rookie of the year on all the polls and get most of the ink. But it's doubtful whether Coach Coryell and especially Dan Fouts, would deal J.J. for any other player in the league.

As for the Chargers, they finished the year with a winning, 9–7 record, going 8–4 under Coryell and missing the playoffs by a margin of a single victory. If they had just beaten one of the weaker teams they went flat against. And then there was the first Oakland game, when the Raiders scored in the final seconds on a fluke offensive fumble which was slapped across the goal line, then recovered for a score.

"It really hurts to think about that play," said J.J., "and the other games we blew. But I don't think many people thought we'd bounce back the way we did. They know we're a playoff team and what's more important, we know it."

Though Campbell might have been the most publicized rookie of the year, J.J. nevertheless made all the All-Rookie teams, some of the All-Pro teams, and was named to play for the AFC squad in the Pro Bowl. So his immense talents were not exactly a secret around the football world. He had established himself quite nicely, thank you. After all, he led the entire league in touchdown catches and was the first rookie since Bob Hayes in 1965 to go over the 1,000-yard mark in receptions. No one could ignore that kind of record.

J.J. had some rather important business to take care of in the off season. He was married. His bride

was the former DeWanda Johnson, his high school
sweetheart, and they still make their home in Dallas.

But soon J.J. was thinking about football again,
and how to make the top passing offense in the
entire NFL even better. The rookies were asked to
report to camp a week ahead of the veterans, and
when they came, there was J.J. right with them.

"I think it's good for me to be here," J.J. explained. "It isn't like we have the same offense as
last year. Coach Coryell is putting in a whole new
system, different passing formations, new blocking
assignments, everything. I think it's very important
to know all this to the letter."

Some of the sportswriters covering the team
couldn't believe it, that a guy like J.J. was coming
in for extra work. After all, he had dropped just
one pass as a rookie, and that was on the play
which separated his shoulder. But you don't get as
good as J.J. by resting on your laurels. And he was
setting a great example for the young players.

There was one rookie who really excited J.J. as
well as everyone else. His name was Kellen
Winslow and he was from the University of Missouri. Winslow stood 6–5 and weighed 250 pounds.
But the best thing about him was that he played
tight end! Winslow was cut from the new mold of
tight ends, a big strong kid, but one with the speed
to go deep. He would give an already potent passing attack still another dimension.

J.J. was as excited as everyone else about
Winslow joining the team. "I've been telling everyone that we got the best football player in the
draft," he said. "I played against him in college
and I know what he can do."

Everyone was high on the upcoming year. Quarterback Fouts put it pure and simple: "We're going to throw the ball," he said, "and we don't care who knows it."

It was a brazen, but prophetic statement. For over the course of the next two seasons, the Chargers were going to unveil the most potent passing attack the NFL had ever seen. The pieces were falling into place almost perfectly. Quarterback Fouts was an accurate, explosive passer, with incredible full-field vision. If one receiver was covered, he had the knack of picking up the others in an instant and getting the ball there with his quick release. Then there were the receivers.

J.J. was the focal point, the gamebreaker, the guy who could catch short and long, and make the clutch catch with the game on the line. Veteran Joiner was a precision pattern runner, a gutty competitor who made up with brains and moves what he lacked in speed. He was especially effective when the defense couldn't key on him, and with J.J. and now Winslow, they couldn't. Plus the second-string receivers were also effective.

As training camp got underway, J.J. took more of an active leadership role, and especially tried to help the rookie Winslow. When Kellen pulled a hamstring in camp and couldn't practice, it was J.J. who tried to lift the rookie's spirits.

"Kellen feels guilty because he can't practice," J.J. said. "When I hurt my eye last year I felt the same way. But I told him he can't let himself feel guilty, but had to try to take a positive view of the whole thing.

"I also told Kellen that catching the ball every time isn't so important. What's important is being where you should be, and that's why you've got to know all the patterns and formations as second nature. You've got to execute perfectly, yet automatically."

The team was just 2–2 in preseason, but spent a good deal of time working on new plays and giving the new players a chance to perform. The veterans got in shape at their own pace. When the season was set to begin it was obvious to everyone that the Chargers were going to be tough, a definitely possibility to go all the way. And some of his veteran teammates were beginning to compare J.J. with the best they had ever seen.

Said running back Lydell Mitchell, in the league since 1972. "People talk about Lynn Swann and those guys," Mitchell said, "but I think John is the best. He's young, but he's the best. The sky is the limit for him. He has a knack for catching the ball wherever it is, an innate knack. Yet he's disciplined in his patterns and can catch the ball in the middle."

Backup quarterback James Harris, who came into the league in 1969, had also seen many of the great ones of the '60s and '70s.

"If we lost John we'd be taking the best receiver in football out of the lineup. It would really have an effect on us. Charlie Joiner is one of the smartest receivers in football and there are other guys who can do a good job. But John is the one who lets us dictate certain things to the defense.

"He's got a great feel for the passing game. Even experience isn't that important a factor with him. He's always been a receiver and he's had a feel for all the adjustments he's had to make. He always gives 100 percent and plays hurt. What more could anyone ask for?"

Though there were some injuries at the outset of the season, the team nevertheless won an easy,

33–16, victory over Seattle in the opening game. J.J., Joiner, and young Winslow all caught a pair of passes in a relatively modest beginning. But the following week they began opening up. They beat the hated Raiders, 30–10, as J.J. scored the game's first touchdown on a 24-yarder from Fouts. He had five catches for 76 yards to lead the receivers. Game three brought still another win, 27–19, over Buffalo, as running back Clarence Williams gained 157 yards and scored all four Charger touchdowns. For once, the passing game stayed relatively quiet.

Then came a big one with powerful New England. At the beginning, it looked like one of the Chargers periodic letdowns. By the middle of the second quarter the Patriots had a 20–0 lead. But the Chargers didn't quit. First J.J. grabbed a 19-yard scoring pass to make it 20–7. Williams scored to make it 20–14, but New England held together and went up by 27–14 early in the final session.

Once again the Chargers steamed back. Williams scored again to make it 27–21, and with time running out, San Diego had the ball once more. They moved in close and Fouts looked for J.J. in the end zone. He saw him and fired. What he didn't see was Patriot linebacker Steve Nelson, who picked the ball off to end the threat. New England held on to win, 27–21, as the Chargers lost for the first time.

"We were just a pass away," said J.J., who had snagged four for 59 yards. "I was thinking touchdown, but Dan just didn't see Nelson. If he had, he could have lofted the ball higher and I still could have gotten it. But it's one of those things. At least we didn't lay down and die once they got the lead on us. Last year, I don't think the team would have come back like this."

Even though the Chargers were at 3–1, they

hadn't been overwhelming in the passing department. It seemed as if they were ready to explode on someone. It started the next week with a 31–9 victory over San Francisco. Fouts threw for 251 yards and Winslow began to fulfill his potential with seven catches for 72 yards. J.J. had another modest afternoon, with four for 52.

The next game was something of an enigma. Fouts threw for 305 yards and the Chargers moved up and down the field all afternoon. They did everything but score. Denver beat them, 7–0, as four missed field goals didn't help. Joiner had seven catches for 115 yards, while J.J. got four for just 48. Those numbers were not up to his standards.

Then came Seattle and once again Fouts filled the air with passes. He completed an amazing 28 of 35 for 318 yards as San Diego won, 20–10. This time his primary target was J.J., and the second-year pro responded with nine grabs for 137 yards and two scores, the final one coming on a beautiful 49-yarder. Now the team seemed to be rolling, but there were some who began saying the team was out of balance, that they were throwing too much and couldn't win the big ones without a balanced attack. The past few weeks the running game seemed to be neglected.

But the club wasn't going to abandon its hot ticket right now. Playing archrival Los Angeles, Fouts opened it up again. With the score tied at 7–7 in the second period, he wound up and hit J.J. with a bomb, covering 65 yards for the go-ahead score. From there the Chargers rolled. They had a big third period and went on to a 40–16 victory. When it ended, Fouts had 326 yards, his third straight 300-yard game. Joiner caught seven for 168 yards and J.J. had three for 112. With Winslow hurt and out of the lineup, the two wide receivers were doing a great job.

A week later Fouts set a new record by throwing for 300 yards in his fourth straight game. He had 303 on 21 of 37, but the defense broke down and Oakland won going away, 45–22. J.J. caught another bomb, a 57-yarder for a score and had four catches for 109 yards, while Joiner had nine for 107. It had been J.J.'s third straight 100-yard game, and Joiner's second. If they could do it once more, they'd tie a record achieved just once, that is, two receivers each grabbing passes for more than 100 yards three straight games.

More importantly, though, was the team's 6–3 record after nine games. They were leading the AFC West and hoping for their first division title since the merger in 1970. They had also scored 233 points, most in the AFC, and the passing attack was averaging 242.6 yards a game, and that was the best in the entire National Football League. Yet there were still people who insisted the club could only go so far without a running attack. They pointed out that during Fouts' four 300-yard games, the club lost twice.

But Coryell and Fouts were committed to passing and weren't about to change, not with J.J., Charlie Joiner and the rest playing so well. But Winslow was lost for the year. He had broken a bone in his leg in the seventh game against Seattle. To that point, the rookie had 25 catches. He'd be hard to replace.

After nine games, both J.J. and Joiner had 35 catches each, tied for fourth best in the AFC. And J.J.'s six TD's were tops along with two others. But the most important thing was winning, and that's what the club did against Kansas City, taking a

20–14 decision. Fouts still put the ball in the air 48 times, but threw short most of the day and neither J.J. nor Joiner hit the 100 yard mark this time.

Victories over Cincinnati, Super Bowl champ Pittsburgh, and Kansas City followed, giving the team a 10–3 mark and bringing them closer to a playoff berth and divisional title. In the Kansas City game, J.J. worked his special kind of magic once more.

The score was tied at 7–7 late in the second period, as the Chiefs were playing the Chargers even to that point. San Diego was at the K.C. 42 and Fouts sent J.J. down the sideline on a fly pattern. The quarterback threw and for a second it looked to be long. But J.J. dove and stretched his arms out, barely catching the ball on his fingertips as he sprawled into the end zone. It gave the Chargers the lead and they went on to win it, 28–7.

After the game, Fouts said this about J.J.'s grab. "You know, that's about as good a catch as you've ever seen. Most receivers *want* to make a catch like that. The difference with J.J. is that he *expects* to make those kind of catches."

As usual, J.J. downplayed his efforts. "I didn't think it was spectacular, really," he said. "Maybe it was one of my better catches since I've been in San Diego, but I've had harder catches in high school and college. I've caught them sliding, I've caught them one-handed and all sorts of things. On this one, once the ball hit my hands it was just a matter of pulling it in."

The club was upset the next week, Atlanta beating them, 28–26, but Fouts had 338 yards and J.J. 103 on the receiving end. Then came an easy, 35–0, victory over New Orleans, a game in which J.J. caught his 10th TD pass of the season and also

went over the 1,000 yard mark for the second
straight year. The win gave the team an 11–4 record,
but they still had to beat 10–5 Denver in the finale to
win the divisional crown.

And there was still another problem. J.J. came
out of the New Orleans game with a rib injury. He
sustained it at the end of the second period while
grabbing a 22-yard pass to set up the Chargers'
final score. X-rays showed no crack or fracture,
but he was still doubtful for the game. The team
was assured of a playoff berth, but they wanted to
win the division and not be the wildcard team.
Whether to risk J.J. became an important question.

Finally, the decision was made not to use him
unless it was absolutely necessary. For awhile it
looked as if he'd have to play. Denver took a 7–0
lead in the first period. But the Chargers came back
to tie before the half, then went ahead in the third
period as Joiner caught a 32-yard TD pass from
Fouts. A field goal in the final session put the icing
on the cake and the defense did the rest. The
Chargers won, 17–7, finishing with a 12–4 record
(matched only by Pittsburgh in the rest of the
league) and taking the AFC West.

There was a dramatic moment near the end of
the game. Joiner had gone over the 1,000-yard
mark in receptions and J.J. joined him at midfield.
The two joined hands and held them high over
their heads as the huge crowd screamed with excitement.

It had indeed been an exciting year. Quarterback
Fouts tied a record by having six, 300-yard games,
and broke another with 4,082 yards for the season.
J.J. had wound up with 61 catches for 1,090 yards
and 10 touchdowns. His per catch average was
17.9, the same as his rookie year, and his stats were

all comparable. It was an amazingly consistent performance. The veteran Joiner chimed in with 72 catches for 1,008 yards and four scores. They were quite a duo, as quarterback Fouts attested.

"J.J. is the finest receiver I've ever thrown to," he said. "He has the ability to be the best in the game. As for Charlie, he probably has the finest knack for getting open I've ever seen. He has a great feel for the game. It's almost like he has a built-in sonar or something."

In his two years in the league, J.J. had so many compliments that all the adjectives used to describe his skills would probably fill a book. And in all that time, there wasn't one bad or negative word said about him. Yet no matter how much success he achieved, he never stopped working. The important thing was for the team to win. Now they were in the playoffs and had a chance to go all the way.

By winning the division, the team had a bye the first week while the two wildcard teams in each conference fought for survival. In the AFC, Houston played Denver in a tough game. When it ended, the Oilers took a 13–7 victory, but it was a costly one. Fullback Earl Campbell, quarterback Dan Pastorini, and star wide receiver Ken Burrough all went down with injuries and were extremely doubtful for the game with the Chargers the following week.

With the game in San Diego and the announcement that both Campbell and Pastorini would not play, the Chargers became prohibitive favorites to win and go on to the AFC title game. Early in the first period San Diego got the ball on its own 19 and started driving. This time, Dan was mixing the run and pass, and the drive was a solid one.

The Chargers pushed the Oilers all the way upfield to the one, and Clarence Williams went over for the first touchdown of the day. They made it look so easy that their fans even relaxed. Without Pastorini and Campbell, how could the Oilers come back?

But the Houston defense suddenly began turning things around. Suddenly, the Charger offense wasn't moving. Early in the second period the Oilers moved in for a 26-yard field goal. Then, minutes later, safety Vernon Perry intercepted a Fouts pass at the San Diego 38. Houston drove in for a score and took a 10–7 lead in at halftime. It was hard to believe what was happening.

Early in the third period the Chargers began moving again. They embarked on another long drive, with Fouts hitting key passes to J.J., Joiner, and tight end Bob Klein. Lydell Mitchell got the score, running the ball over from the eight. The kick made it 14–10, Chargers. Perhaps now they were ready to take control of the game.

But keen observers of the Chargers noted that Fouts was not real sharp. His was not throwing with his usual confidence and pinpoint accuracy. He was going to have to be very careful. Late in the third period he threw one poorly again. J.C. Wilson intercepted at the Charger 49. Three plays later quarterback Gifford Neilson hit Mike Renfro on a 47-yard touchdown pass that put the Oilers back on top, 17–14.

In the fourth period the Chargers began getting worried, and Fouts was putting the ball up even more. The Oilers gave him some short ones, but when it got serious, they were waiting. Their defense continued to dominate. Free safety Vernon Perry wound up the defensive star with four interceptions and a block of a field goal try. The

Chargers just couldn't put anymore points on the board. They wound up losing, 17–14, and were eliminated from playoff contention.

It was a difficult blow to take. Incredibly, Fouts had thrown for 333 yards on 25 of 47, but there were five interceptions. More critics began saying a team couldn't win throwing *that* much. There was just too big a margin for error.

None of the receivers was really able to dominate. J.J. had four catches for 70 yards, but didn't score. Joiner had four for 81, running back Williams had four, so did Lydell Mitchell, and tight end Bob Klein grabbed five. That wasn't the way they usually did it. The wide receivers were generally the big catchers. But the Houston defense deserved a lot of the credit for stopping them.

It's hard to say why the Chargers were derailed, especially by an Oiler team at less than full strength. According to one writer, lack of playoff experience did them in. Many people maintain that the playoffs in all sports have a special kind of intensity, and that teams coming in for the first time often get caught short. As the 1980 preseason was ready to roll, this same writer added:

"Now, after learning their lesson, the Chargers have all the necessary components to make a strong run at the Super Bowl."

That seemed to be the consensus opinion of most. The one possible gap was the continued lack of a strong runner who could establish a dominant running game. But Fouts was pulling the trigger again, he still had J.J. and Joiner, and a healthy Kellen Winslow looked ready to contribute in a big way.

J.J., of course, was a seasoned veteran by now, though as enthusiastic as ever. When he was held out of the first two preseason games he was literally chomping at the bit. Finally, Coach Coryell unleashed him in the third game against the 49ers. San Francisco won the game, 17–14, but J.J. showed the inactivity hadn't changed him one bit. He grabbed eight passes for 122 yards and a touchdown.

"I really felt out of it for awhile," J.J. said, "but I understand the situation here. We have a couple of receivers trying to make the club and the coaches have to see them play. That's fine with me. I'd rather let them have the chance. We've got a pretty good crop of rookies, but time is winding down for them. Some of them will have to play again in the final exhibition next week. That's fine with me, too."

By the time the 1980 season opened, the Chargers looked like a well-oiled machine once again. They demolished the Seattle Seahawks, 34–13, with Fouts going upstairs for 230 yards and J.J. the prime target on the other end. He caught touchdown passes of 10 and 23 yards and wound up the day with six catches for 103 yards. The man could play ball.

The next week it was Oakland and this would be the first real test of the year. These two teams always slugged it out like a pair of heavyweight fighters, and the rivalry went all the way back to early AFL days. In the first period, neither team could really get it going and on an exchange of field goals left it deadlocked at 3–3.

Then in the second period the Chargers began moving. They took it all the way down to the four. Still, Fouts wanted to pass. He looked for J.J. and fired toward the rear of the end zone. J.J. made a leaping one-handed catch against all-pro cor-

nerback Lester Hayes for the score. The kick made
it 10–3, but Oakland came back to tie it at halftime.

The Raiders got the only score in the third period on a recovered fumble and run, but Fouts was
again racking up yards in the air and J.J. was putting together another big game at his end. The
topsy-turvy action continued in the fourth. The
Chargers tied it again as Winslow hauled in a 25-
yard TD pass. Then they took the lead as Williams
ran in from four yards out. But the Raiders tied it
as Raymond Chester caught an 18-yard scoring
toss from Jim Plunkett. It was 24-all at the end of
regulation. Now it was sudden death overtime.

Each team tried to get moving a couple of times,
but the defenses held. Finally, the Chargers got
something going. They moved into Oakland territory and were threatening. They had the
ball on the Raider 24, but it was a third down and
11 play. Coryell wanted to try a field goal, which
would win it. But offensive coordinator Joe Gibbs
had already called a pass play.

Fouts dropped back and looked for—who
else?—J.J., who was running down the left side
with Lester Hayes on him. When Fouts fired, both
J.J. and Hayes looked back and each lost the ball
in the bright afternoon sun. But it was J.J. who
picked it up first, leaped, and made another one-
handed grab. He hit the ground at about the one-
yard line, but since Hayes hadn't touched him, he
rolled over into the end zone for the winning score.

The catch capped a brilliant afternoon. J.J.
grabbed nine passes for 110 yards and the two
brilliant TD catches. He looked to be better than
ever.

"There was a real glare from the sun out there,"
J.J. said. "I could see the ball coming, then I lost it.

But I had a pretty good idea of where the ball was going. I just put up my right hand and the ball kind of stuck. I knew I had it once I got my hand on it."

That was J.J., making the spectacular seem routine. Lester Hayes, on his way to a brilliant season, thought it was a little more than routine.

"I'm all over the guy and he still catches the ball," said Hayes. "Two really sensational catches. What are you gonna do about a guy like that."

Even with the great win, there was criticism. Fouts had set a club record with 29 completions and 387 yards. But he had also thrown five interceptions and there were those who felt the Chargers were going to live and die by the pass once more. Against Oakland, even with J.J.'s nine catches for 110 yards, he wasn't the leading receiver. Tight end Winslow, coming into his own, had nine grabs for 132 yards. So Fouts had even more weapons to work with now.

The Oakland game was J.J.'s 31st as a pro, and with the constant comparisons to Lance Alworth which had gone on for three years, one writer decided to make it more direct. After 31 games, J.J. had 27 TD catches, the same as Alworth had after 31 games. J.J. had caught 132 passes compared to 130 for Alworth. Alworth did have the lead in yards per catch, 20.4 to 17.5. And when somebody contacted Alworth to get his opinion of J.J., the former Charger was happy to comply.

"He's a fantastic player and I love watching him," Alworth said. "He's very fortunate, as I was, to be with a team that exploits his talent. That makes the whole thing work. He could have gone to a team that didn't throw much and not had the same opportunity to catch the ball.

"I must admit that I do see myself somewhat in

J.J. and I can easily relate to him. He'll go into a crowd across the middle, knowing he's going to get hit, but he goes ahead and does it. He has great concentration and always goes after the ball. I used to feel, when I went after a ball, that it was mine. I see the same thing in J.J."

The more people who compared the two seemed to think there were great similarities. And Alworth is regarded as one of the most spectacular receivers of all-time.

It was back to the well the next week with another easy win over a good team, a 30–13 defeat of Denver. Then Kansas City fell, 24–7, as the Chargers ran their record to 4–0. Later that week it was announced that the team had made a deal that many people felt would bring them a championship. They acquired running back Chuck Muncie from the New Orleans Saints. Muncie was a 6–3, 235-pound power back who had the speed to run outside. He had gained nearly 1,200 yards for the Saints in 1979, but had fallen into disfavor in New Orleans.

If Muncie could regain his past form, he could give the Chargers the one thing they lacked, the big running game. The question was would Coryell and Fouts alter their game plan to utilize Muncie's talents? Only time would tell. At this point the team was still unbeaten, so they had to be doing something right.

The next week it was the battle of unbeatens as the Chargers met the surprising Buffalo Bills. San Diego led 24–12, after three, but allowed Buffalo to tally twice in the final session to win, 26–24. Muncie played, but wasn't much of a factor, while J.J. had seven catches for 85 yards and a score. But the loss to the Bills wouldn't hurt as much as the one the following week.

It was another epic battle with the Raiders, the game in doubt until the final quarter when Oakland halfback Kenny King sprinted 89 yards for a score. The final was 38–24, and the Chargers lost more than a game. Offensive tackle Russ Washington fractured a kneecap and would be lost for the year, while defensive tackle Louie Kelcher hurt a knee and might miss six weeks.

Despite the loss, it was another aerial circus by Fouts and company. The QB threw for 388 yards, Joiner caught eight for 135, Winslow seven for 91, and J.J. five for 114. It might sound like a maze of repetitive statistics, but it shows how the Chargers were en route to becoming the passingest team in the history of the game. They almost had three receivers catching for 100 yards each. And Fouts just kept putting it up.

Take the next game, for example. It was against the lowly New York Giants, and the San Diego quarterback threw for the incredible total of 444 yards in a 44–7 romp. More stats. Joiner had 10 for 171 yards, Winslow six for 102, and J.J. five catches for 107 yards, including a 39-yard touchdown. They were quickly becoming the most devastating trio of receivers in league history.

A week later the club lost to Dallas in a high-scoring donnybrook, 42–31, as the Cowboys dominated the second half, 28–7. The team was now 5–3 after eight games, tied with Oakland and just a game ahead of Denver, Kansas City, and Seattle, all of which were at 4–4. So it was anybody's ballgame and the Chargers had lost three of four.

But they kept throwing. Fouts had 371 yards

against Dallas and J.J. starred with eight catches for 160 yards, including a 58-yard TD bomb. With the season half over, J.J., Winslow, and Joiner ranked one, two, three among AFC receivers. And they were catching at a record-setting pace. They also helped each other whenever they could.

"Charlie took me under his wing and taught me how to read defenses so fast," said J.J. "It was a good feeling that someone I had admired for so long would help me. A lot of guys would shy away from a number one draft choice thinking they might lose some of their own publicity and notoriety if the young guy got too good. But Charlie never did and I'm grateful for that and always will be."

And Joiner was just as quick to talk about his running mate at wideout. "When J.J. came into the league, he was no rookie," the veteran said. "He's also the most coachable young receiver in the game and plays as if he already has 10 years experience. He's way ahead of the other receivers his age. In fact, I'd say that right now J.J. is the best receiver in the league."

As for Winslow, also having an all-pro year, he was thankful for having both J.J. and Joiner playing alongside him.

"Being able to play with two such great receivers has been so important to me," he said. "Most of the time I draw single coverage because they concentrate on those two. And believe me, I don't mind that at all."

Now it was time for the second half of the season, and the team opened it with an easy, 31–14, win over Cincinnati. Winslow was the big man again, with nine catches for 153 yards. His stats for a tight end were really imposing, and the Chargers often used an offense with just one running back, a second tight end in Greg McCrary, leaving Winslow to act as a third wide receiver with the other two. The team could move through the air, no doubt about that.

But suddenly, another upset. Denver surprised the Chargers, 20–13, handing San Diego its fourth loss in six games and knocking them out of first place in the AFC West. As had been the case in too many recent losses, Fouts had a great day statistically, with 363 yards. Joiner caught nine of them for 127, and Chuck Muncie had his first big day on the ground with 115 yards on 23 carries. Look at the stats and you wonder how the team could lose. Some people began wondering if perhaps something was missing, say an intangible, like character or knowing how to win. They certainly weren't doing it against the better teams, and for the first time all year, a playoff spot was in some doubt.

The team didn't need just a win now, they needed some kind of a streak. A 20–7 victory over the Chiefs might be a start. They followed it up with an overtime win against Miami, 27–24, and for the second game in a row they had a good balance between the run and pass. In some ways, the team seemed to do better when Fouts threw for only about 250 yards. Those real big passing days always seemed to find the team in trouble.

Now came a big test against the Philadelphia Eagles, who were coming in with the best record in the league, 11–1. The Chargers jumped all over them in the first half. Winslow caught a 14 yard scoring pass. Rolf Benirschke kicked a 34-yard field goal. Winslow caught another from 17-yards out, and J.J. was catching everything in between. It was 19–0 at the half.

But in the second half the Eagles came on. They made it 19–7, before another Benirschke field goal made it 22–7. In the final session the Eagles got two more scores and came very close, losing 22–21. It was a big victory for the Chargers and a milestone for John Jefferson.

On the very first play of the game, J.J. had hauled in a 50-yard bomb from Fouts, and that catch put him over the 1,000 yard mark again, making him the first receiver in NFL history to get 1,000 yards receiving in each of his first three seasons in the league. On the day, he had eight catches for 164 yards, his sixth 100-yard game of the season. Fouts threw for 342 yards, his sixth, 300-yard game of the year, tying his own record of a year earlier, a record shared with Joe Namath, the former great quarterback of the Jets.

Later in the same game, Winslow also went over the 1,000-yard mark, and Joiner was just 53 yards away. They were still one-two-three in the AFC and the club was back in first with a 9–4 mark. So it looked as if the team was back on the beam, but the next week the roof fell in again.

The Chargers were humiliated by a Washington Redskin team that entered the game with a 3–10 record. The final score was 40–14 and San Diego was never in it. Fouts had a poor day, throwing five intercepts, though he became the first QB in league history to go over 4,000 yards for a season twice. But this was not his day. J.J. caught just two, Winslow one and Joiner three. Those aren't Charger statistics. The team was now tied with Oakland at 9–5, and critics again wondered if the club would ever find the consistency to become a champion.

A 21–14 victory over Seattle followed, and now it

came down to the final week of the season. The
Chargers didn't play until Monday night, when
they would be meeting the powerful Pittsburgh
Steelers. By then, they knew everything was on the
line. Oakland had finished at 11–5. A Charger win
would also put them at 11–5 and give them the division title because of their record within the AFC
West. But a loss would drop them not only to 10–6,
but out of the playoff picture completely. Houston
and New England would be the wild-card teams.
So it was all riding on one game before a national
television audience.

It was a defensive battle in the first half. San Diego scored on three field goals, the Steelers one,
making it 9–3. There was an exchange of touchdowns in the third period plus another San Diego
field goal. Each team got one more score in the
fourth and the Chargers had taken a neat, 26–17
victory. They had done it. Fouts had another
record-breaking 300-yard day, and Winslow closed
with 10 more catches for 171 yards. He had become
awesome.

What a year it had been for the Charger passing
attack. Fouts set records for completions, attempts, and yards, with 348 of 589 for an incredible
4,715 passing yards. And his three receivers also set
marks. Winslow led the NFL in catches with 89, a
record for a tight end, and he gained 1,290 yards to
go with nine touchdowns. Veteran Joiner had 71
catches for 1,132 yards and four scores.

But once again the most spectacular receiver of
them all was John Jefferson. J.J. had 82 catches
(remember when he said defenses were too tough for
70-80-catch seasons?) for a league leading 1,340
yards. And once again he paced the NFL in touchdowns through the air with 13. And if someone

kept the stats, he probably led the league in circus catches once more. He was already great, but still getting better.

Now to the matter of the playoffs. The Chargers would be meeting the AFC champion, the Buffalo Bills, a surprise team all year. On paper, the Bills didn't look that powerful, but they gave the Chargers a tough game.

San Diego got a field goal from Benirschke in the first period, but then the Bills took over. They scored twice in the second to take a 14–3 lead at the half. In the third period they got one back when Fouts hit Joiner from nine yards out. Then in the final session another Benirschke three-pointer made it 14–13, but the Chargers still trailed.

Finally, midway in the final session the Chargers had the ball and moved it to midfield. Tight end Greg McCrary had gone out earlier with a back injury, negating the two-tight-end offense and cutting Winslow's effectiveness somewhat. So with the ball on the 50, the Chargers sent substitute wide receiver Ron Smith in the game. He lined up on the right side, while Jefferson, Joiner, and Winslow all went left.

Fouts dropped back, and with the defense concentrating on the three stars, he pumped a 50-yard touchdown pass to the seldom used Smith. The kick made it 20–14, and that's the way it ended. The Chargers had won their first playoff game. Fouts had 314 yards passing, Chuck Muncie gained 80 on the ground, and J.J. led the receivers with seven catches for 102 yards. It was a good game, but now there would be a bigger one, a showdown with Oakland for the AFC title and a trip to the Super Bowl.

The way these two teams had battled the past

several seasons, this one was sure to be a war. The
Raiders took the opening kickoff and on their third
play from scrimmage, quarterback Jim Plunkett
threw a short pass over the middle for halfback
Kenny King. The ball popped out of King's hands
and was grabbed by tight end Raymond Chester,
who took off and caught the surprised Charger defense flatfooted. He ran 65 yards to the end zone
and Oakland had a sudden, 7–0 lead.

Midway through the period the Chargers tied it
on a 48-yard pass from Fouts to Joiner. Then the
Raiders took over. A 76-yard drive resulted in a
Plunkett score at 11:14 of the period. San Diego
had to punt on its next possession and Oakland
marched in again, 49-yards on just four plays. At
the end of a quarter the Raiders already had a 21–7
lead.

Oakland scored again midway through the second to make it 28–7, and it looked like the Chargers
were disappearing without a whimper. But before
the half they drove 64 yards, Fouts hitting key
passes to J.J. for 10 yards, running back Mike
Thomas for 24, then finding Joiner in the end zone
from eight yards out. It was now 28–14.

That seemed to bring the Chargers back to life.
In the third period a 68-yard drive resulted in a
field goal, as J.J. caught a key, 19-yard pass on the
drive. Then, minutes later, a 28-yard punt return
gave the Chargers the ball on the Oakland 41. They
drove downfield and Muncie scored from the six.
Suddenly, they were back in it at 28–24, with
momentum on their side.

But Oakland broke it with a 68 yard drive at the
end of the period, resulting in a 27-yard field goal
and a 31–24 lead. Still, the game was up for grabs as
the final session began. When the Raiders got an-

other field goal at 5:14, they had a cushion with a 34–24 lead.

The Chargers drove again midway through, but all they could get from the march was another Benirschke field goal, bringing it to 34–27, with nearly seven minutes left. But after that it was all defense. Neither team scored again and the Raiders had won a trip to the Super Bowl. The Chargers were beaten once more.

It was a familiar pattern, Fouts throwing for 336 yards, but the team losing. There were some injuries, like Muncie leaving with a hurt shoulder, but that's no excuse. The question will continue over whether the team should change its offensive philosophy, but that will be difficult with the kind of receivers they have.

J.J. didn't have a real good game against Oakland. He caught four balls for 71 yards, but a couple bounced away from him that he normally would have nailed. The Raiders must have breathed a collective sigh of relief when they saw that, because they have been burned by J.J. before.

So has just about everyone else around the National Football League. No receiver of recent years has made catches of the spectacular variety such as J.J., and he's done it consistently during the three years he's been in the league. And in spite of his overnight success as a rookie, he's worked hard to keep improving, and done it with enthusiasm and good humor. He's still basically the same confident and mature kid who came out of Roosevelt High in Dallas some eight years ago.

"Football is more of a job now than it was in high school or college," J.J. said, recently. "We put in some long hours, but game days are still fun. After a week of hard work, that's when you test your skills. And when things work out, it's still a real thrill."

J.J. has had many real thrills and given an equal number to the many football fans who have watched him perform. But perhaps the nicest thing about it all is what lies ahead. With John Jefferson, it is a pretty safe bet that the best is yet to come.

★ Earl Campbell ★

Of all the positions on a football team, running back is probably the easiest in terms of the transition from college to pro ball. That doesn't mean it's easy to be a runner. But the runner, more so than other players, is doing what comes naturally.

Quarterbacks must learn a whole new offensive system and become familiar with new personnel, as well as learn to spot and read all kinds of defenses. Receivers have to learn new pass routes and develop a sense of timing with their quarterback and with other receivers. Linemen must learn new blocking techniques as well as their exact assignment on each different play. Defensive players must learn to work as a unit, to stunt and blitz, and to cover for each other. They've got to recognize changing offensive formations and know what their jobs are with each variation.

But a running back, he just runs, using his speed, his power, and his cutting ability to follow blockers as he has done all his football life. Sure, he must learn his plays, know where the holes are, and which way his blockers like to go. And it's true that he must work on other facets of the game, such as blocking and pass receiving. But as far as pure running is concerned, it's not that difficult a transition for the talented back.

Of course, a runner needs help. He's got to have an offensive line and a complementary passing game behind him. Take O.J. Simpson, for instance. To many, he's the greatest running back ever to play the game. But his first few years in Buffalo, behind an anemic offensive line and a team that was always playing catch-up football, were pure torture.

Then there are the players who come in from college, make the quick transition to the pros, and play well. But in a few years they're done, either victims of injury, the constant battering, or the lack of enough extra talent to keep them a step ahead of the defenders.

So while the transition isn't difficult for a runner, there are still only a few with the immense talent that makes them superstars. Young halfbacks coming into the league invariably find themselves compared with either O.J. Simpson or Gale Sayers, while the bigger men, the fullbacks, are generally compared against a single standard, the great Jim Brown.

Brown was perhaps the first power runner who also had the speed and moves of a halfback. He could bull his way for the short yardage, and also go outside to break a big one like a halfback. Speed and power, that was the classic combination that Brown brought to the game, and now every young fullback who shows flashes of greatness is compared with the great Cleveland Browns' immortal.

In the National Football League of the middle 1970s, the fullback who comes closest to possessing

the classic combination of skills is Franco Harris of
the Pittsburgh Steelers. Franco is a fine runner, an
outstanding fullback who is over 1,000 yards nearly every year. He's got inside power and is a dangerous cutback runner who uses his blockers well
and has the speed to outrun the secondary once
he's there. But Franco is not really a "moves"
runner.

Then, in 1978, the Houston Oilers got a rookie
fullback out of the University of Texas, who also
happened to be the Heisman Trophy winner of
1977, the best college player in the land. His name
was Earl Campbell, and it wasn't long before the
comparisons were being made.

The regular season hadn't even begun when
Houston center Carl Mauck said ths about
Campbell:

"I hate to beat the drum too soon on Campbell,
but he's reminding me more and more of Jim
Brown. And Brown, to me, is the best who ever
played the game. Earl has all the power he needs.
He can run like a deer, too. When he gets out in the
open with a 180-pound defensive back, it's a bad
mismatch."

Mauck admitted he was beating an early drum,
but he had reason to. At 5'11", 225 pounds, Earl
Campbell was a powerhouse. He had thick, piston-
like legs that gave him tremendous thrust and
drive. Plus he had the quickness to hit the hole and
the cutting ability that most big men don't possess.

And he wasn't coming out of nowhere. He had
just completed a great career at Texas, where he
had led the nation in rushing his senior year before
winning the Heisman Trophy. He came out of col-

lege with one of those "can't miss" labels, which sometimes puts everyone's expectations too high, and also can serve to give the player the proverbial swelled head.

But that wasn't the case with Earl. He knew what it meant to come from humble beginnings, having been raised by his mother along with ten brothers and sisters. So he was a man of singular purpose—to become the best he could possibly be at his chosen profession.

And unlike a lot of top stars, Earl Campbell was well liked by everyone, one of the most personable and popular athletes of his time. Despite his college credentials, his primary objective was to blend in, be part of the team, and do all he could to contribute to that team's success.

He was joining a pro team that had been in the pits for a long time. The Oilers weren't exactly a doormat, but they were the kind of club that could never seem to get over the hump. They would come close . . . then blow it. So when a mammoth deal was completed to give the Oilers the draft rights to Earl Campbell, he was viewed as a savior, a man who would supply the missing ingredients to make the Oilers a playoff team. The pressure was really on as Earl went into his rookie year in the National Football League.

How did this youngster from a small Texas town, one of 11 children raised in near poverty, ascend to the pinnacle of the football world? Let's find out.

Earl Campbell was born on March 29, 1955, in Tyler, Texas. He was the fifth of 11 children born to Ann and B.C. Campbell. There were seven boys and four girls. Mr. Campbell supported the family as best he could by taking odd jobs here and there and by growing roses. That's why one of Earl's nicknames when he played for Texas was "The Tyler Rose."

Earl's mother had lived around Tyler all her life. She grew up in Smith County, which was about seven miles from Tyler. As a girl, she was bussed to the all-black Emmett Scott High School in Tyler. Three weeks after she graduated in 1942, she married B.C. Campbell and began raising her family.

The Campbell home in Tyler was a gray, weather-beaten frame house, described by Mrs. Campbell as "down-the-years tired." It was located at the end of a winding road some five miles north of town. On one side of the house was an old peach orchard, and on the other an automobile graveyard filled with wrecked and rusting cars. At first glance it was sometimes difficult to tell if anyone lived in the house or not.

The Campbells moved into the house in late 1965, when Earl was just ten years old. His father planned to fix the place up in his spare time. But he was busy working and tending the rose garden, which the kids helped him with by hauling water and doing other chores.

Then one afternoon, about six months after they moved into the house, Mr. Campbell came in from the rose field and told his wife, "I'm just sick." He was having a heart attack. They took him to a hospital and nine days later he died. Mrs. Campbell remembers that well.

"When I came home from the hospital the day my husband died the children had already heard the news," she said. "Earl was sitting by himself right out on the front porch. He looked up and told me, 'Mama, now that this has happened, let's have the funeral and get it over with.' "

Earl's instincts were right. As tragic as losing their father was, the family didn't have time to mourn, not with 11 children to be clothed and fed. So Mrs. Campbell had to make a big decision.

"I could have walked off and left," she said. "But I decided I was going to hold my family together, and that's what I did. I sat them all down and talked to them. I told them I was by myself now and I had to have their help. I couldn't afford to pay their fines if they got put in jail. If they got in trouble with the police, they'd just have to take care of it themselves.

"And you know, I never had to pay one fine, either. Now I'm not saying they didn't get any fines. But if they did, they sure kept it out of my ear."

So Mrs. Campbell got to work. She continued to work the 100-acre rose field with the help of the children, and she took jobs as a maid wherever she could find them. She also found help from God. Being very religious, she passed this along to her children as well, and every Sunday they attended the Hopewell Baptist Church.

By this time Earl was already playing football with his friends. It was always his favorite sport, and many a time when he was supposed to be working in the rose field he was in the yard throwing a football around instead, much to his mother's chagrin.

When Earl was getting ready to enter John Tyler

High School, his mother tried to discourage him from playing football.

"Part of it was my protective nature. I didn't want to see Earl get hurt," his mother said. "And if he did get hurt, there was no money to pay for doctors' bills."

But finally Mrs. Campbell gave in and Earl went out for the football team. He was a running back and linebacker as a sophomore, and he played very hard. A Houston sportscaster remembers working as a newspaper reporter back then and seeing Earl play as a soph.

"I covered one of the first games he ever played at John Tyler," the man said. "He sacked the quarterback eight times while playing linebacker. But after the game he wasn't happy because the other team had completed too many passes over him. Earl was always criticizing himself, even then."

Earl had a pretty good sophomore season at John Tyler. But he wasn't a dedicated football player then. In fact, he was beginning to drift slowly toward a different type of life, with different types of friends. His off-field activities were becoming more important to him, and they weren't the activities of a model citizen.

"By then I was smoking a pack of cigarettes a day," he admits, "doing a little hustling with a pool cue, shooting craps, drinking—the whole number. I didn't spend one minute thinking about the future. I figured one day I'd get out of school, get me a car, and bum around. My friends called me 'Bad Earl,' and I was on the path to the penitentiary."

His junior year as a football player was pretty

much of a bust. It just didn't seem to matter to him. It all came to a head the day of that year's final game. John Tyler was slated to play crosstown rival Robert E. Lee High. But that morning Earl wasn't in school. He and four of his friends, also ballplayers, were bumming around town. Someone spotted them and they were suspended.

That's when Ann Campbell stepped in again. She had had enough. She told Earl that he was setting a bad example for his younger brothers and sisters, and reminded him that she could barely make ends meet and wouldn't be able to help him if he got in trouble. She also reminded him of some positive things he was throwing away.

"My Mom brought me to a realization that changed my life," Earl says. "She told me that I was something special, that God had given me a talent. She said I could go on and use that blessing, get an education, and play professional football. But I couldn't do any of that if I kept on doing what my friends were doing."

So in the summer of 1973, before his senior year, Earl rededicated himself to football. He gave up smoking, drinking, and bumming around. He worked out incessantly, getting himself into the best shape of his life. He was already strong and muscular, with great quickness and agility. When school started in the fall he always ran the four miles home instead of taking the bus. And when the season started he was ready.

He ran like a man possessed. His speed and strength were the talk of the league, as he ran over and around and through people, time and again, gaining huge clumps of yardage and leading John Tyler to a great season. He was already a bruising, punishing runner who often left would-be tacklers sprawled on the field behind him.

Incredible as it may seem, Earl rushed for 2,037 yards his senior year, and despite the fact that he was playing for a rather obscure high school, his fame spread rapidly. Before long recruiters from major football schools all around the country were flocking to the old frame house in Tyler. Picking a college wouldn't be an easy decision for Earl and his family.

All the recruiters and coaches gave Earl and his mother their pitches, promising all kinds of things if Earl went to their schools. That sure didn't make things easier. Earl's grades were also a concern, but he worked very hard his senior year to attain the C average he would need under NCAA rules to play varsity ball as a freshman.

Just when the Campbells seemed to be in a complete quandary about their choice of a school, Darrell Royal came along. He was the head coach at the University of Texas, and as soon as Earl and his mother met him, they liked him. Coach Royal was a sincere and charming man, who made it a point to go right out to the Campbell house and talk to them in person.

"He sat right there on that couch," Mrs. Campbell told a reporter later. "And he was my favorite from the beginning. He was just fantastic. I guess I just liked his style."

So did Earl, and he liked the sound of the football program at Texas. He also liked the campus and the facilities, which he saw on a visit to Austin.

That clinched it. He signed a letter of intent to become a Texas Longhorn in the autumn of 1974.

By enrolling at Texas, Earl would be going to one of the most prestigious and tradition-bound football schools in the country. The Longhorns had been fielding teams since 1893, most of them quite successful. Upon Earl's graduation in 1977, Longhorn gridders had compiled an all-time record of 570 wins, 207 losses, and 29 ties. The school had ten unbeaten, untied seasons, and had won the national championship three times. They were in the Southwest Conference and played a rugged schedule.

Needless to say, Earl made the team as a freshman and found himself starting in a backfield that included another big power runner, Roosevelt Leaks. Leaks was no slouch. In a game against SMU the year before, he had run for a phenomenal total of 342 yards. He was expected to be Texas's main man, with Earl in a supporting role.

It didn't work out that way. A knee injury put Leaks on the shelf, and Earl soon found himself the big back. In his very first varsity game against Boston College he carried the ball 13 times and gained 85 yards, an average of 6.5 a pop, as the Longhorns won, 42-19. Even in his first game his tremendous power was in evidence, and the B.C. defenders had a hard time containing him.

Texas had a fine team that year and Earl made an immediate impact. In the fourth game, against Washington, he powered and slashed his way to 125 yards on just 16 carries. That's almost eight yards a try. He had three more 100-yard games that year, including 127 yards in a workhorse 28 carries in the season finale against archrival Texas A&M. The Longhorns won that one, 32-3, to finish the regular season at 8-3. A loss to Auburn in the Gator Bowl dampened things a bit, but it was nevertheless a fine year and an outstanding first year for Earl.

In 11 regular-season games, he rushed for 928 yards on 162 carries, an average of 5.7 yards a try, and he scored six touchdowns. He was definitely a player to be reckoned with.

By now Earl was thinking of football and the future. He was resolute in what he wanted. He was determined to do his best for his team at Texas, and then go on to the pros. "I want to make enough money someday to build my mama a house, so that when she goes to bed at night she won't see the Big Dipper," he said.

Coach Royal was also aware of how serious a person and performer Earl was.

"There is little room for nonsense in his life," said the coach. "He's too busy trying to make something of himself. I'm not saying he walks around with his brow wrinkled all the time. He loves to laugh. It's just that he's not generally the fella who is making the laughter."

In his sophomore year of 1975, Earl really blossomed. He gained 103 yards in his first game against Colorado State, then came back against Washington to gain 198 on 27 carries with three touchdowns. He followed it up with 150 against Texas Tech on 18 carries, adding another pair of touchdowns. He was getting national headlines and being touted as an All-America candidate. And he was now something of a celebrity around the Austin campus. He was constantly besieged by youngsters wanting to talk to him or ask for an autograph.

"When I was a kid working in the rose field," he said, "I couldn't understand why so many bad things were happening to me. Now everytime a little kid comes up and I sign an autograph for him, I'm trying to repay a little of what I owe."

It was an enviable attitude. Earl had become a quiet, sincere, appreciative person. The wild ways of his high school days were a thing of the past. His mother said she began to relax when she learned that Earl and a date were asked to leave an Austin bar once—for drinking only orange juice instead of alcohol.

After most games, Earl would return to his room instead of celebrating. His fellow Longhorns began calling him "the father of the team," but they all had tremendous respect for his ability.

An out-of-town writer noted that on one play he could run like a "Mack truck, and on the next like a runaway gazelle." He was still a punishing runner, using his powerful legs to churn through people, and his tremendous upper body strength to deliver blows with his shoulders and arms. Yet he was an extremely clean player who would never try intentionally to hurt someone, although getting in his way when he had the football could be risky. Yet his overall attitude and demeanor was evident when he asked a writer one day:

"Have you ever seen a man who doesn't get mad?"

"No," the man said.

"Have you ever seen a man who doesn't know

how to get mad?" Earl asked next.

"No," the man said again.

"Well," said Earl, "you're looking at one now."

Earl continued his fine play. He had two more big games, getting 160 yards against SMU and 133 against Baylor. When the season ended, he had gained 1,118 yards on 198 carries for a 5.6 average and 13 touchdowns. Texas was nationally ranked with a 9-2 record, and Earl was an All-American, having been named on several post-season polls. He proved it was a good choice by being named the outstanding offensive player of the Astro-Blue-bonnet Bowl that year, as the Longhorns rolled over Colorado, 38-21.

Most people figured Earl would be better than ever in 1976. It wasn't known then, but it came out later that Earl had not been happy with the Wish-bone offense that Coach Royal and the Longhorns used. In the Wishbone, there are three backs behind the quarterback, with the fullback the closest to the signal-caller, instead of being the deepest, as in other formations. Earl apparently felt he could be a more effective runner and help the team more if he lined up deep. But that would have meant another kind of offense, and Coach Royal wasn't about to change.

It was a young Longhorn team that reported for the 1976 season. Several key players had graduated, and there were inexperienced underclassmen at several key positions. Earl was back, of course, looking bigger and more imposing than ever. He *was* bigger, in fact. His weight was up to about 245 pounds. Yet he still seemed to have his speed. To many, he looked unstoppable.

But in the first game that year, the whole team was stopped. Boston College pulled perhaps the upset of the decade by whipping the Longhorns, 14-13. Earl was held to just 23 yards on five carries. The entire offense had a terrible day, and the team was a big question mark as it went up against North Texas the following week.

If it had not been for the running of Earl Campbell, this one might have gotten away, as well. Texas won 17-14, largely because Earl ran wild, having the first 200-yard day of his career. He rambled for 208 yards on a workhorse 32 carries, scoring one touchdown and dazzling everyone with a brilliant, 83-yard run. Despite his added weight, he still seemed to be moving extremely well.

After an easy win against Rice, the team then played a hard-fought, 6-6 tie with archrival Oklahoma. Earl had a busy day with 91 yards on 27 carries for a 3.4 average, below his usual standard. He then got just 57 yards on 17 tries in a 13-12 squeaker over SMU. Suddenly he did not look like the same runner who had had that sensational 208-yard day a few weeks earlier.

In fact, he wasn't the same. He was having leg problems—hamstring problems to be exact—that were beginning to slow him up. Against Texas Tech, Earl managed to run for 65 yards on seven carries. It looked like he was going to have a big day. Then the leg went completely. The team lost that game, then three of the next four, and in those games Earl was out for the first time in his career.

He returned for the final game against Arkansas and seemed to be his old self, carrying 32 times for 131 yards and two touchdowns as the Longhorns won, 29-12, somewhat salvaging a dismal 5-5-1 season, their poorest showing in more than 20 years.

Earl missed four games outright and parts of a couple of others. His seasonal stats read 653 yards on 138 carries for a 4.7 average. He scored just three touchdowns. There were no All-American honors this time, and some people began wondering if the leg injuries would become chronic.

Shortly after the season ended, an announcement came out of Austin. Darrell Royal was stepping down as head coach after 20 years. Royal would remain as athletic director, and the new head football coach would be Fred Akers, who had been Earl's backfield coach his freshman year of 1974. Akers had then gone to Wyoming as head coach for two years and was now returning to Texas. Earl had been one of Akers's favorite players three years earlier, and when he returned to Texas, Akers joked about the big runner.

"The only difference in Earl Campbell as I remember him as a freshman and now is about 4,000 yards."

But there were a few problems that Earl had to deal with before his senior year. There were his leg injuries. Earl took a step toward helping himself when he discovered that wearing a thin pair of pantyhose under his uniform gave him that little extra support he needed.

"I have big legs," said Earl, "so it kind of holds them together. Instead of my legs shaking, it holds them steady, supports them."

Another problem was Earl's weight. Coach Akers asked him to lose about 20 pounds, to get back to 225. He felt Earl would be just as effective as a power runner, would be a bit quicker, and would be less likely to suffer a recurrence of the leg pulls.

Back home in Tyler, Earl went on a diet. And he also began to talk with friends about the past season. He reportedly told people that he was fed up with the Wishbone offense, that he couldn't be as effective a runner using it, and that it was also responsible for his getting banged up as a junior. In addition, he found that a number of people, who had been patting him on the back during his fine sophomore season, hardly spoke to him as a junior. This, too, upset Earl, though he was learning that there's always a what-have-you-done-for-me-lately attitude among some people in sports.

Earl's depression didn't last long. He soon learned that Coach Akers was scrapping the Wishbone. He would replace it with the Veer and the I-formation. The Veer has just two running backs behind the quarterback instead of the three in the Wishbone. In the Veer, Earl would run from the halfback slot to take more advantage of his quickness. In the I-formation, the two backs line up one behind the other. The deep back is called the tailback and is usually the big yardage runner. Such great backs as O.J. Simpson and Tony Dorsett ran out of the I as collegians and gained huge chunks of yardage.

Earl reported to practice in great shape. He was back to 225 pounds, wearing his pantyhose, and raring to go. Some thought it would be a rebuilding year, but Texas had a lot of mature talent. They would be a very quick team.

The team had a couple of other potential superstars besides Earl. There was defensive tackle Brad Shearer and placekicker-punter Russell Erxleben. Wide receiver Alfred Jackson was also an outstanding player, as was offensive guard Rick Ingraham. There were also a number of younger players of vast potential, such as running back Johnny "Ham" Jones and receiver Johnny "Lam" Jones, who had been an Olympic sprinter in 1976.

So the team had a number of outstanding players who didn't get much publicity. Plus, Earl's twin brothers were also on the team. Tim Campbell was a defensive end and returning letterman, while Steve Campbell was a back-up linebacker. That, too, made Earl happy.

The longhorns opened the 1977 season against Boston College, the team that had upset them a year earlier. This time Texas came out flying. They buried B.C., 44-0, as Earl cruised for 87 yards on 17 carries. But it wasn't until the following two weeks that Texas showed it was a much different team than in 1976. This Longhorn outfit had devastating striking power, and at the hub of the attack was a rejuvenated Earl Campbell.

First came Virginia, a team totally incapable of dealing with the juggernaut that hit them. Texas won the game, 68-0, as Earl served notice that he was back with 156 yards on 19 carries. His longest run was just 20 yards, so he piled his total up very evenly in the course of the afternoon.

Then came Rice University. In this one, the Longhorns scored ten times in 14 possessions. Erxleben set a new NCAA record by booting an incredible 67-yard field goal, and Earl ran for 131 yards on just 13 carries. He tied a school record by scoring four touchdowns as the Longhorns rolled, 72-15, and people began talking about the great job first-year coach Jack Akers was doing in Austin.

Game four would be a big one. The Longhorns would be meeting mighty Oklahoma in the Cotton Bowl in Dallas. Texas had not beaten the Sooners since 1970, although they came close in '76 with a 6-6 tie. This time they wanted the win.

Oklahoma took an early lead in the first quarter on a 47-yard field goal. But early in the second period Erxleben topped that by booting one from 64 yards out to tie the game. Then late in the period Texas began driving from its own 20. Earl was eating up big chunks of yardage against the tough Sooner defense. Finally with the ball on the 24 he burst through a hole in the line, faked a linebacker, and ran past a startled secondary into the end zone. The kick made it a 10-3 game at the half.

The final two periods were mainly a defensive struggle. Oklahoma got a 32-yard field goal in the third, and then the big foot of Erxleben split the uprights from 58 yards out in the final session, giving the Longhorns a 13-6 victory and moving them closer to the top in the national rankings. Earl had rushed 124 yards on 23 carries for a 5.4 average against the stingy Sooner defense. He was now being touted as perhaps the best running back in the country and a possible Heisman Trophy winner.

Then it was archrival Arkansas, giving the Longhorns their second stiff test in two weeks. Again it was the defenses that stood out. In the first half Erxleben booted field goals of 58 and 52 yards while Steve Little of Arkansas kicked one from the

33 and then tied Erxleben's record by hitting from 67 yards out to make it a 6-6 game at the half. Little hit from the 25 in the third period to give the Razorbacks a 9-6 advantage.

In the fourth period Earl was controlling the game with his running, as he had earlier, but the Arkansas defense tightened when it had to. Finally, late in the session, Texas began driving from its own 20. Earl ripped off some nice gains in between passes to Ham Jones and Alfred Jackson. Finally from the 29, quarterback Randy McEachern dropped back and hit Earl over the middle. The big guy ran it all the way down to the one.

From there, Ham Jones took it in and Erxleben's kick made it a 13-9 game. That's the way it ended, and the Longhorns remained unbeaten.

Despite the fact that it was a low-scoring, defensive battle, Earl had put on a fantastic show. He carried 34 times for 188 yards, a 5.5 average, and along the route had become the top ground-gainer in Southwest Conference history. There didn't seem to be any stopping him.

A week later he did it all over again, topping himself, in fact, with a 213-yard performance against SMU. He carried the ball 32 times and scored a touchdown as Texas won again, 30-14. He had a 58-yard touchdown run in the game that showed the essence of his talents, as he used both his power and speed, leaving Mustang tacklers all over the field.

"Earl was incredible today," said Coach Akers. "He's been incredible all year. I can't imagine a better all-around running back anywhere, college or pro. He's got as much power as I've seen in a back, yet when he gets open, no one can match him. His combination of leg and upper body strength makes him awfully hard to tackle, and when you do bring him down, you know it."

The Texas steamroller continued. Texas Tech, Houston, TCU, and Baylor all fell easily, as Earl continued to ramble, picking up 116, 173, 153, and 181 yards in the process. He was the nation's leading runner and looked like a good bet to cop the Heisman. In addition, the Longhorns were now 10-0 and the top-rated team in the country. Only one regular-season game remained, the traditional clash with Texas A&M.

It was a tough Aggie team that went against the Longhorns in the season finale. But they were no match for the devastating striking power of Texas. And they just couldn't find a way to stop the thunderbolt that was Earl Campbell. The Aggies scored first early in the game, marching 70 yards after the opening kickoff. But after that it was all Texas.

The first time Texas got the ball they worked it up to their own 40. Then quarterback McEachern dropped back and lofted one downfield for Earl, who had come out of the backfield. The big guy caught the ball on the dead run and rambled all the way into the end zone to complete a 60-yard pass-run touchdown play.

It was the first of five straight touchdown drives in the first half for the Longhorns. Earl was the bulwark of each one, running with abandon, knocking tacklers out of his way, faking others, and not going down until there were three or four players hanging on his back. At halftime it was a 33-14 game.

Texas A&M tried to rally in the third period, and the score became 40-28. But in the final session Earl and his teammates put it on again, scoring 17 more points and rolling to a 57-28 triumph to close the season with a perfect, 11-0, record.

And in that final game Earl outdid himself. He ran 27 times for a career-high 222 yards and four touchdowns. And he finished the season as the nation's leading rusher with 1,744 yards on 267 carries for a tremendous 6.5 average. How many so-called power runners can average that much a pop? In addition, Earl scored 19 touchdowns to lead the country in scoring.

For his Longhorn career, Earl ran for 4,443 yards on 765 tries, for a 5.8 average. He was, of course, the all-time Texas rushing leader as well as the all-time Southwest Conference running king. Needless to say, he was a consensus All-American being named on every team in the land. He was also an odds-on favorite to win the coveted Heisman Trophy.

Earl came to New York in early December for the Heisman Trophy ceremonies. The winner would be announced at the award dinner. Someone asked Earl's mother what she thought about her son's winning the Heisman, and Mrs. Campbell once again showed the strong moral fiber that was present in this unusual family.

"I still don't know what this Heisman business is really all about," she said. "People ask me about it and I tell them if Earl gets it, then that's nice. If he doesn't, then being runner-up would be nice, too. I just hope it is given in the right spirit."

One thing was sure. It was given to the right

man. When the winner was announced, the name of Earl Campbell surprised no one. And Earl was a gracious winner. He noted that he brought a teammate with him, guard Rick Ingraham, because "he made a lot of holes for me at left guard."

Then he showed his appreciation for all his mother had done by asking her to stand for everyone in attendance to see. He then told the large gathering that he would "represent what a Heisman trophy winner should be."

In his closing remarks, Earl said, "Everybody has dreams. A lot of times you wake up and the dream is not there. This is the dream come true to me."

Earl also told reporters that he wanted to go on to a successful pro career.

"I'm confident I can play," he said. "When the time comes I'll go out there and do my best. That's about all I can do. If the Good Lord wants me to have something, then I'll get it. But whatever happens, I'll always be a Longhorn, just like I'll always be from Tyler."

Earl was saying he'd always remain the same person, no matter what kind of success or failure he found down the road, and no matter how much money he made. He also said that the first thing he would do when he signed a pro contract would be to buy his mother and his family a new house. Mrs. Campbell, of course, was asked what she thought about Earl's plans.

"I've given that some thought," she said. "The people who lived in this house before we did had 11 children, too, so there's been 22 kids come through here. It won't be easy to leave. But if Earl would like me to have something better, I do think I could enjoy being just a *little* more comfortable."

Being in New York for the Heisman, Earl soon found himself besieged by agents who wanted to represent him in his pro negotiations. But Earl said that would have to wait. He had another game to play for Texas. The Longhorns had a date in the Cotton Bowl with Notre Dame. They would have to win one more time to be national champions.

It turned out to be a game the Longhorns would have liked to forget. The Fighting Irish had a strong team, with mammoth offensive and defensive lines. They used their bulk and strength very well on this day and neutralized the speed of the Texas team. In addition, the Irish offense was clicking behind quarterback Joe Montana. The Longhorns were never in it. Notre Dame won big, 38-10, in an upset that gave the Irish, not the Longhorns, the national championship.

It was a bitter way for Earl to end his college career, but that single loss could not dim his great achievements in 1977 and his fine play for Texas since 1974. Now it was time to look to the future and professional football.

The pro football draft traditionally has the poorest teams picking first and the best last. It's a system that is supposed to give the league a chance to balance out. Therefore the top college players often find themselves on the weaker teams. It happened to O.J. Simpson when he had to go from sunny California to ice cold Buffalo and a cellar-dwelling team.

Only a trade can change the scheme of things. In the 1977 draft, the two expansion teams of 1976,

Tampa Bay and Seattle, had the first picks. Tampa Bay picked USC running back Ricky Bell, primarily because Bell's old college coach, John McKay, was now at Tampa. Bell, incidentally, had been an outstanding college runner.

Seattle was then ready to pick the '76 Heisman winner, running back Tony Dorsett of Pittsburgh. But right before the draft, the Dallas Cowboys gave Seattle a number of players and draft choices for the rights to Dorsett, so Touchdown Tony started his career with one of the NFL's finest teams and wound up with a Super Bowl ring his rookie year.

This was the kind of speculation that centered around Earl. Tampa Bay had the first pick again, and there wasn't any doubt about who the most valuable college player was. But then again a player like Earl could bring an expansion team like Tampa Bay three or four first-line players.

At the same time there was talk about keeping Earl in his native state. That would mean either the Dallas Cowboys or Houston Oilers would have to make a deal to get him. Dallas, of course, was a powerhouse. The Cowboys had been at or near the top for a decade, having gone to the Super Bowl four times and winning it twice. People in Cowboyland envisioned a backfield of Campbell and Dorsett, the two greatest college runners of the '70s.

But the price would be high. To get Dorsett the Cowboys had not needed to part with any of their established stars. With Earl it might be different. The price might just be too high.

Houston, on the other hand, had a greater need.

The Oilers were a strange team. They were born into the old American Football League in 1960 and were one of the AFL's best in those early years. But since the two leagues had merged in 1970, the Oilers had never been in the playoffs.

During the last several years, the team seemed to be improving, but they would always lose a key game, sustain a key injury, or just plain blow it. In 1977, the team finished at 8-6, a game behind Pittsburgh in the AFC Central Division. They missed the playoffs by a single game.

The club was solid at many positions. Their quarterback was a strong-armed thrower from Santa Clara, Dan Pastorini. Pastorini was one of those quarterbacks who could never seem to get past the "potential" stage. He had all the physical tools, but never seemed able to enter the elite class of NFL signal-callers.

Some said he was bomb happy, unable to stick to a game plan. He had an All-Pro wide receiver in Ken Burrough and some other fine pass-catchers. The problem, supporters said, was that Pastorini never had the running game to support his passing. This could be cured by the addition of You Know Who!

The Oiler defense was young, tough, and getting better. There were standouts such as linemen Curley Culp and Elvin Bethea, and linebacker Robert Brazile. The team's coach was the colorful "Bum" Phillips, who always appeared on the sidelines in a huge cowboy hat and fancy western boots. This was the team that made no secret of wanting Earl Campbell.

"I'd watched Earl on film," said Coach Phillips,

"and I thought he was the best back in college football and maybe the best in a long, long time. There's no doubt that we wanted to see him in a Houston uniform."

The speculation continued. Then, shortly before the draft, the deal was announced. Houston gave Tampa Bay their first-and second-round draft picks for 1978, their third and fifth picks in '79, plus second-year tight end Jimmy Giles. In return they got the league's first draft pick and used it to grab Earl Campbell. The Tyler Rose would stay in Texas.

Earl was overjoyed to be staying in his home state. He knew there would be pressure on him to produce, but he felt he was ready to deal with it.

"I think the most important thing this year is that I come out every day and do my best on the football field," he said. "I just want to go out and do my best. If my team wins, I want to be part of it, too."

But before Earl would wear the Houston uniform, there was the matter of his contract. His agent was Mike Trope of Los Angeles, and he negotiated a five-year, $1.38 million pact for Earl. There were also other fringe benefits befitting a number one draft choice. He began endorsing some products, from athletic shoes to snuff. He made some TV commercials for several businesses in the Houston area and taped a testimonial for another product. But once practice started, it was all football.

"The other stuff was fun," Earl said. "But the fun's over now. I'm not really into that the way I am football. Football determines whether I eat or not. I've got to zoom in on one thing. It's tough learning a new system."

Earl began working hard to learn the Oilers' plays and players. He wasn't in any way a prima donna. As far as he was concerned, his immense college credentials and his awards now meant nothing. It was what he did now, how hard he worked, and what he could contribute to the team that counted. He wanted no part of a fancy, baby blue Continental Mark V, a luxury car he was offered with a very liberal payment plan. He preferred to drive the van his friends from Tyler had given him.

"Earl's got such a low profile," said backfield coach Andy Bourgeois. "He is unlike most Heisman Trophy winners who wear flashy clothes, buy big cars, and lead pretty fast lifestyles. Earl's profile is about as slow as he walks. He's got two speeds—crawling and exploding."

The only sign of his new wealth was a modest three bedroom house he bought for himself in southwest Houston. And he also fulfilled his life-long ambition of getting his mother a new home, also a three bedroom home, back in Tyler.

On the field he was easing himself into the team slowly. Many hot-shot players coming into the pro league make a big deal of getting their old college number. Not Earl. He wore number 20 at Texas, but that number was worn by two-year defensive back Bill Currier. It didn't matter to Earl, who donned number 34.

"Bill can keep his number," he said. "Just as long as I've got a number, that's fine. I don't think it's the number that slips you through a hole, anyway."

Earl patiently answered reporters' questions and was embarrassed by their constant attention. He didn't want it to look like he was getting all the attention while his teammates were neglected. And his low profile was appreciated by the veteran players. Elvin Bethea expressed it when he said:

"We appreciate that Earl didn't come in here with his mouth open. The guy has got a good head on his shoulders. A lot of guys who come in under that kind of pressure will never make it. But Earl will. It seems like he's been through it before."

Earl also got a new nickname during camp. Whenever he was tackled he always got up slowly and ambled back to the huddle in a very weary fashion. One day defensive end Jim Young saw him and said, "Hello, Easy Earl!"

But Easy Earl was working hard and was very intense about his football. He stayed after each practice and did extra work on his pass-receiving, since he had been used very sparingly in that capacity at Texas. And some nights he could be found on the dormitory parking lot walking through new plays with a few offensive linemen.

"I'm kind of restless at night," he said. "Sometimes I close my eyes and see myself running plays. I'm not worried. But I want to learn them right, and I'm anxious to get on the field and play."

His aggressiveness increased as the pre-season approached. In some early practices he was up against players who wouldn't make it, the fringe guys who would be cut. Bum Phillips noticed that Earl took it easy with some of them.

"He just wouldn't take advantage of that kind of situation," said the coach. "He could have run over some of those people to show his strength, but he didn't."

Yet he showed enough to impress everyone. One man who loved his style was backfield coach Andy Bourgeois.

"Earl's more of a flasher than a jitterbugger," said Bourgeois. "For that reason, he really fits well into our offense. His explosiveness, his balance, his shoulder strength and leg strength are quite obvious. After working with him just two weeks, it was easy to understand why he won the Heisman."

And Oiler scout Bill Groman compared him with the two top rookie runners of a year earlier, Tony Dorsett and Ricky Bell.

"Earl has Bell's power to go through a tackler and Dorsett's quickness to elude one," was the way Groman put it.

In the team's first rookie scrimmage with Kansas City, Earl gained just 38 yards on ten carries. He looked a bit unsure of himself and was also upset by mishandling a couple of passes.

"We probably should have gone ahead and given him the ball 35 times," said Coach Phillips. "I guarantee you he would have done something in those 35 carries to show why he's the Heisman winner. Like I've said all along, he's not a one-play back. He's a bunch-of-plays back. Just wait and see."

It never comes that fast to a rookie. But with Earl it just seemed like a matter of time. Then in the team's first pre-season game with Denver, Earl got just 29 yards on 12 carries as the team lost, 17-12. That was not typical Campbell, and some of the players involved talked about his performance.

"He's got a lot of talent, but he's also got a lot to learn," said Denver defensive end Lyle Alzado. "The holes won't be the same as they were at Texas. Sometimes, he'll just have to take charge and go."

Denver linebacker Joe Rizzo seemed a little disappointed. "Campbell didn't hit the holes as fast as I thought he would," he said.

One of Earl's teammates, tackle Greg Sampson, thought Earl would still have to make some adjustments.

"He has to learn to get through the tunnels we set up for running plays," said Sampson. "He has to do the old thing about running for daylight. You can't just barge in there with quick hits."

His slow progress notwithstanding, Earl was already having a positive effect on Oiler fortunes. Since his signing, season ticket sales had gone up to some 44,000 from the 29,600 of a year earlier. And the Texas State Network, which broadcasts the Oiler games, expanded from seven stations to 66. So from that standpoint, Earl was already well worth the big investment.

Two weeks later he started paying dividends on the field. The Oilers had a pre-season game with the Dallas Cowboys, a game billed as the Pro Football Championship of Texas. And all of a sudden Earl Campbell was running wild. The Cowboys couldn't seem to stop him as he reeled off one big gain after another.

At one point he sprung loose and showed the classic combination of speed and power in racing for a 55-yard touchdown. Later he cleared the way for a Ronnie Coleman touchdown by throwing a brutal block on Cowboys' safety Cliff Harris. Harris is one of the roughest, toughest players in the league, but Earl cartwheeled him as if he were a pencil. When the game ended Houston had a 27-13 victory, and Earl Campbell had run for 151 yards on 14 carries. That's better than ten yards a pop.

"I've always said I'm never satisfied and that I want to do better," Earl said afterward. "But I guess I'm pretty happy with the game."

As for Cliff Harris, he knew he had been steam-rolled by quite a player.

"He's big and fast," said the Dallas safety. "I didn't give him enough credit. I didn't know what he could do. But now I know. In fact, he's one of the best I've ever faced during my time in football."

Later, center Carl Mauck slapped Earl on the back and congratulated him on a great game. Earl's answer was characteristic.

"Hey, man," he said. "I couldn't do it without you guys. You blocked real well. I was right on your tail on that touchdown and you know it."

The game was no fluke. It was just a preview of things to come. In the season opener, Earl was more than ready. Playing against Atlanta, the rookie ran like an All-Pro. The Falcons saw early on that they couldn't stop him, so they concentrated on the rest of the Houston offense. Earl's NFL debut resulted in a 137-yard day, on just 15 carries. But the bottom line was that the team lost, 20-14.

"Sure, I'm happy with my performance," Earl said. "I didn't expect to do so well. But it doesn't really matter because we lost. To tell the truth, I'm not concerned about how many yards I get. My biggest goal this year is to play and stay healthy the whole season and to help this team to win."

The next week Earl was over 100 yards again, getting 107 on 22 carries against Kansas City. This time the Oilers won, but it took a sudden-death overtime and a field goal to give then a 20-17 final. The Chiefs were not considered a strong team at all, and people began wondering if it was the same old Oilers again.

Another squeaker followed, 20-19 win over a very poor San Francisco team. Earl had 78 yards on 25 carries in this one, and even more people began to have their doubts about the Oilers. A 10-6 loss to the Rams didn't help matters. Earl had 77 yards on 13 carries, but he pulled a hamstring again and was a doubtful starter for the following week. Could the season be falling apart already?

Earl didn't play the next week against Cleveland, but the team won, 16-13, to raise their record to 3-2. The next week they played mighty Oakland, and once again a loss resulted, this time 21-17. Every game had been a close one, and the only consolation in this one was that Earl had returned and played very well, running for 104 yards against a very tough Oakland defense. The hamstring pull had been minor and the week's rest had healed it.

But after six games the team was just 3-3 and seemingly struggling. They were struggling in spite of Earl's fine showing that had put him up among the league's top rushers. Earl wanted the team to do better, but other than that had settled into a routine that was not so different from his college days.

"As far as playing in the pros and in college, there has not been that much difference," he said. "I still get hit! In college I would have Sunday and Monday to get myself back together. Then I would be ready to play by Tuesday. In the pros I take Monday and Tuesday to get myself together, and by Wednesday I'm ready to play again."

Next came a victory over Buffalo, 17-10, as Earl went over the century mark once more, with 105 yards on 19 carries. Now it was on to Pittsburgh, where the Oilers would have a pivotal game with the division-leading and unbeaten Steelers. The whole season might just hinge on the Houston showing in this game. If the Steelers blew them out, the team could crack.

Earl would be going up against the rock-ribbed Steel Curtain defense for the first time. It was a defense that had allowed the fewest points in the NFL through seven games. Mean Joe Greene, Jack Lambert, Mel Blount, and company would be out to teach the rookie a lesson. The game was a Monday night TVer, and a huge audience would be watching.

The game was scoreless in the first period, although Earl was running well and often penetrating the Steel Curtain's famous front four. The Steelers took the lead in the second quarter as Terry Bradshaw hit Lynn Swann on a 25-yard TD pass. But the Oilers came back, driving to the one and watching Earl ram in. An exchange of field goals made it a 10-10 game at the half.

Then in the third period the Oilers drove downfield again. This time Earl took it in from the three, the kick giving Houston a 17-10 lead. They upped it to 24-10 in the final session with Earl getting his third score of the game from the one. The Steelers rallied again, as Bradshaw hit Swann from six yards out, making it 24-17, with 5:20 left. Pittsburgh then recovered an onsides kick and drove to the Houston 15. But Kurt Knoff intercepted a Bradshaw pass at the one. A final Pitt drive ended at the 11 and the Oilers had a big win.

Earl had led the way once more, with 89 tough yards on 21 carries.

"I'll tell you this," he said. "I respect the Steelers and I think they played a very clean, physical game. But I knew our offensive line could do a great job of blocking, and they did."

The Steeler defense knew it had a young thunderbolt to contend with. It didn't take Jack Lambert long to become a believer.

"He ran right over the top of me one time," the All-Pro middle linebacker said. "They ran on us tonight like no other team has this season, and Mr. Campbell was the reason. You can see why he was their top draft choice. He's short, low to the ground, and one time down near the goal line, I was standing up, trying to get rid of a guard, and he ran right over me."

So Earl was getting respect, and so perhaps, was the team. The victory brought their record to 5-3, good enough for second place behind the Steelers, and talk of getting into the playoffs started anew.

But the team just couldn't find any consistency. The next week they went up against a Cincinnati team that was 0-8 coming in, and they lost, 28-13, in spite of Earl's 102 yards. Perhaps it was a natural letdown from the week before. But this had happened too often to the Oilers in recent years.

Suddenly the next contest, against Cleveland, had become a "must" game.

The Browns keyed on Earl all afternoon. He still got the tough yardage, but in the fourth period the Browns had a 10-7 lead. On a third-down play with short yardage, quarterback Pastorini faked to Earl, who pulled it off so well that the Browns' defense converged on him. That gave Pastorini a chance to hit tight end Mike Barber with the winning TD pass, giving the Oilers a 14-10 win.

Earl had 71 yards on 19 carries, giving him 870 yards after ten games, the third best mark in the entire NFL. After the game Earl told reporters he was still working hard at other facets of the game, like receiving and blocking. That's why he felt so good about the fake carry that led to the winning score. It was something besides running that he had mastered. Then someone asked him if the excitement of his rookie year had made him forget about Texas days.

"The Texas experience was something," Earl answered. "My two best friends are former teammates, Alfred Jackson and Raymond Clayborn. In fact, all three of us are going to room together at Texas this summer. I'm going back to take some courses for my degree and they are, too."

But that would have to wait. There was still a playoff chase. And the next stop would be New England. It was to be one of the Oilers' key games of the year. The Patriots were leading the AFC East and were considered by many a good bet to represent the Conference in the Super Bowl.

For the first 28 minutes the game was a total disaster for the Oilers. They coughed the football up three times and each time the Patriots recovered and went in to score. With just two minutes left in the half, New England had a 23-0 lead and seemed to have the game wrapped up.

Houston was stopped again right before the half and punted to the Pats. Stanley Morgan fielded the ball—then fumbled it! Houston recovered and went in to score before the half, making it 23-7. But it still looked bleak.

Early in the third period Patriot kicker David Posey tried a 25-yard field goal and hit the upright. Starting at their own 20, the Oilers had a beautiful nine-minute, 80-yard drive that resulted in another score. That made it 23-14. As soon as New England got the ball back they tried a bomb. It was intercepted by Willie Alexander, and the Oilers were on offense once again.

Still playing ball-control football, the Oilers drove again. This time Earl plunged in from the one. The kick was missed, making the score 23-20. The drive was highlighted by a fake field goal and pitch to halfback Rob Carpenter, who got the first down.

With 6:30 left, the Patriots had the ball at the Oiler 42 and a fourth and two. Quarterback Steve Grogan tried a pass, and safety Mike Reinfeldt knocked it down. Houston had the ball again. Led by the running of Earl Campbell, they moved downfield. The drive ended with Pastorini hitting Rich Caster in the end zone. The kick was again missed, but the Oilers had a 26-23 lead. They held it and won, perhaps their biggest victory of the year.

Earl did not have a typical game. He gained just

74 yards on 24 carries for a 3.1 average, well below the 4.9 he had going in. But his very presence might have made the difference. A Boston writer put it this way:

"On paper, Earl Campbell was far from a pearl. But in reality, he was the key man in the Houston Oilers' stunning 26-23 come-from-behind victory over the Patriots. His rushing average was only 3.1, well below his season's norm. But as Dan Pastorini, who completed 12 of 19 second-half passes for 155 yards, maintained, it was the presence of Campbell that seemed to numb the New England defense."

Pastorini himself said, "Earl gives us another dimension. With him around, they just can't come rushing in to play the pass, and those linebackers have to stay around a little longer to see if Earl is coming."

Veteran Elvin Bethea also talked about Earl, and commented on still another dimension of the rookie's presence:

"When we fell behind like this in the past, we used to fold and then keep going downhill," said Bethea. "Then we'd go into the next game and go straight down the hill further. But now we have confidence in our offense, and the offense has confidence in itself. Earl has been an inspiration. When we can get the ball to him, we feel he can do it."

It was obvious that Earl had become not only an integral part of the team, but perhaps the key man in the club's resurgence. He not only provided the offense with the final link, but also helped the defense by allowing the team to play more ball-control football, thus keeping the offense on longer and giving the defense much-needed breathers.

The win over New England gave the club a 7-4 mark and kept them well in the running for a playoff berth. But there was another tough one coming up, a Monday-nighter against the always-dangerous Miami Dolphins.

It was a wild and woolly game, with the huge crowd at the Houston Astrodome going crazy for 60 minutes. It was tied early at 7-7, with Earl having scored the Houston touchdown on a one-yard plunge. A Pastorini-to-Barber pass put the Oilers on top, 14-7, in the second period, but the Dolphins came back to tie as Bob Griese hit Nat Moore for a ten-yard TD. At the half it was a 14-14 game, and the Dolphins seemed to be containing Earl, who had just 44 yards.

But in the second half Earl showed something that only the very great players have—the ability to get stronger and stronger as a game goes on, while everyone else seems to wilt. In the first series of the second half, he carried on four of seven plays, getting many of the 63 yards in the drive and going in from the six. That made it 21-14.

Once again the Dolphins came back, Griese leading the drive and fullback Leroy Harris scoring from in close. It was tied again. Then early in the fourth quarter, Pastorini dropped back to pass from his own end zone. Earl missed a block, and the QB was tackled in the end zone for a safety. It gave the Dolphins a 23-21 lead, and they seemed to have the momentum.

Then Earl took over once more. He spearheaded another drive with bursts of eight, ten, and six yards, running with power and authority. From the 12 he smashed across to give his club the lead once again, 28-23. Then came one of the most dramatic moments of the football season.

Houston had the ball again. They were hoping for a time-consuming drive to kill the clock. The ball was on their own 19 and Pastorini gave the ball to Earl, who ran over right tackle. Suddenly he was in the Dolphin secondary. But as they raced up the sideline, Earl stayed ahead, even pulled away a bit. He went 81 yards for the score, as the cheers in the Astrodome thundered down upon him. Gasping for breath in the end zone, Earl managed a smile as his teammates all overwhelmed him.

His run made it a 35-23 game and negated a final Dolphin touchdown. Houston had another big victory, 35-30, and Earl had his greatest day as a pro, with 199 yards on 28 carries. The big game gave him 1,143 yards for the season, making him the NFL's rushing leader and putting him right behind Don Wood's rookie rushing record of 1,162 yards. After the game all the talk was of Earl.

"Before the game I told Earl we needed four touchdowns from him and that our defense would keep Delvin Williams under 100 yards," said center Carl Mauck. "It was a joke, but it wasn't a joke, if you know what I mean. I knew that if Earl was running the way he could, they wouldn't be on the field long enough to let Delvin roll it up, and it worked out that way, didn't it?"

Pastorini had completed ten of 16 passes for 156 yards, and he too couldn't say enough about his favorite running back.

"Earl is the best back and the best human being

I've ever had the pleasure of meeting," said the QB. "He's a friend, a worker . . . the best. Even if you don't block for him he'll pick up three, four yards a shot because he's a power runner. And with his speed and moves, it's only a matter of time before he breaks one for you."

Coach Phillips also credited Earl with allowing Pastorini to have the best season of his career.

"Dan has got some weapons now," said the coach. "He didn't used to have any, but now he's got a running game and people have to respect that."

Everyone respected Earl, including the opposition. Miami linebacker Steve Towle, was one of Earl's biggest boosters:

"The key to stopping Earl is that you can't try to stop him all at once. I was watching myself on film the week after the game and when I got near him I was trying to deliver a hard blow. I came up short a lot of times, and one time I missed him completely. You just have to grab on and hope one of your teammates comes along. The first guy cannot do it by himself.

"In running backs, there are quite a few who are big, strong, and fast. The thing that makes Earl unique are two things you add to big, strong, and fast: his acceleration and his balance. He has the acceleration of a much, much smaller man. He possesses the ability to hit the hole quickly, and when you get someone his size running that quickly, you never get a clean shot at him."

Then Towle, a close friend, talked about Earl the man:

"I think the first thing that makes Earl the athlete he is, is the kind of person he is. When I met Earl it was not as a Heisman Trophy winner or as a star football player, it was as a person. The thing I was most impressed with was the dedication he has in the things he does. It seems like that type of dedication carries over to the football field."

Earl's 199-yard performance in the Monday night game really focused the entire football world on his talents. This was no ordinary athlete, nor was this another fine football player. He was an outstanding player, an exciting one, a genuine superstar. And when he gained 122 yards on 27 carries the following week against Cincinnati, he broke the rookie rushing record and held his NFL rushing lead. He also led the league in touchdowns with 12, as the Oilers whipped the Bengals, 17-10, to raise their record to 9-4.

There were some other interesting stats brought to light after this game. For instance, Earl had gotten the ball 24 times on third-down, short-yardage plays. He made the first down 18 of those times. And on fourth down plays he had carried four times and run for an average of 12.2 yards a pop on those critical carries.

The next game was against Pittsburgh again, and the Oilers wanted nothing more than to beat the Steelers a second time. This game was played at home and the team was optimistic. In the first period things looked good. Earl was again churning up the yardage. After seven carries he already had 41 yards and seemed on his way to a big day. But that seventh carry, late in the first period, would be his last of the day.

Earl was hit hard by Steeler safety Donnie Shell

and had to be helped from the field. He was in obvious pain and Oiler fans were shocked to silence. He didn't return as Pittsburgh went on to win the game, 13-3. Afterward, it was learned that Earl had a cracked rib.

"Donnie Shell and another guy were coming at me," Earl said later. "I was going to ricochet off the other guy and take Shell on later, but Shell came up quicker than I expected and caught me off balance. It wasn't dirty or a cheap shot."

But the next week Earl was ready. He would play with a protective pad over his ribs, and would have to play in pain. But he would play. And he contributed 67 yards in 25 tough carries against New Orleans in a 17-12 victory that wrapped up a playoff berth for the Oilers. The team then let down a bit in the finale, losing to San Diego, 45-24, as Earl finished his rookie year in fine style with 77 yards on just 14 tries.

It had been a great year for everyone. The team was 10-6, second to the 14-2 Steelers in the AFC Central, but had made the playoffs as an AFC wild card entry. Pastorini had the best year of his career with 199 completions in 368 attempts for 2,473 yards and 16 touchdowns. He completed 54.1 percent of his passes.

As for Earl, he led the entire NFL in rushing with 1,450 yards on 302 carries for a 4.8 average. He also scored 13 touchdowns and was a sure shot for a slew of post-season awards. But first came the playoffs, and the Oilers were optimistic they could go a long way. Their first opponent would be the other AFC wild card team, the Miami Dolphins.

It would be a battle of the walking wounded.

Earl's ribs still hurt, and both quarterbacks were also injured. Pastorini had a variety of ills, including cracked ribs, a shaky knee, a sore elbow, and a hamstring pull. He would wear a cumbersome flak jacket to protect his ribs. Miami's Bob Griese also had bruised ribs and he wore a thick pad and had to take some pain-killing injections.

The first half was a defensive battle. Both teams scored first-period touchdowns before a scoreless second period. At the half it was a 7-7 game, and Earl had gained just 16 yards. But in the second half, Earl and Pastorini began controlling the game. Houston dominated the third period, but couldn't score. Neither did the Dolphins, as Griese's injury seemed to be taking its toll.

In the fourth period the Oilers began driving. Pastorini completed four straight passes before Tony Fritsch booted a 35-yard field goal. An intercepted pass at the 50 started another drive. This time it was Earl controlling, the big play being a 20-yard sweep around right end. Earl finally went over from the one, and the Oilers had a 17-7 lead. A late intentional safety gave the Dolphins two more points, but it ended at 17-9. The Oilers had won.

Pastorini had a great day with 20 completions in 29 attempts for a whopping 306 yards. Earl bounced back in the second half to finish with 84 yards on 26 carries. Halfback Tim Wilson added 76, as the Oilers rolled up 455 net yards to just 209 for the Dolphins. Now it was on to New England to play the high-scoring Patriots.

The Pats were a troubled team. Their coach, Chuck Fairbanks had been suspended and then reinstated by owner Billy Sullivan, after it was learned that Fairbanks had accepted a job to coach the University of Colorado the following season. So New England was a team in turmoil, and that could only help the Oilers. Plus their quarterback, Steve Grogan, had a sore knee and might not be able to go the distance.

After a scoreless first period, the Oilers began to flex their muscles. Early in the second period Houston got the ball on its own 29. Pastorini threw a pass to Ken Burrough in the left flat, and the speedy receiver sidestepped a Patriot defender and suddenly found himself all alone, streaking down the sidelines for a 71-yard touchdown play. The kick made it a 7-0 game.

Midway through the period the Oilers seemed to have their backs against the wall. They had the ball on their own one-yard line. But now Earl began to ramble, punishing the Pats with hard, determined runs. Four times the Oilers converted on third-down plays, the first of which came on a roughness penalty. Then with the ball on the Patriot 19, Pastorini hit end Mike Barber for the score. Fritsch's kick made it 14-0.

Still, the Oilers weren't finished. Grogan could not move the Pats, and late in the session Houston got the ball on its own 49. Seven plays later Pastorini was hitting Barber again, this time from 13 yards out. At the half it was a 21-0 game, the Oilers in charge.

In the second half back-up quarterback Tom Owen rallied the Pats. Before that Fritsch had booted a 30-yard field goal after ten straight running plays, including a nifty 35 yarder by Earl. But

Owen came on to pass for two scores and narrowed the margin to 24-14, with about eight and one-half minutes left.

But the next time Owen started his team moving, he made a mistake. His overthrown pass was intercepted by the Oilers who brought the ball to the New England 18. Three plays later Earl burst across the goal line from the two, putting the game on ice. Houston won it, 31-14, and now they would go to the AFC title game with . . . who else but Pittsburgh!

Once again it was Campbell and Pastorini who had led the way against New England. Earl was tremendous, a powerhouse with 118 yards on 27 carries, while Pastorini, again ignoring his injuries, hit on 12 of 15 for 200 yards. But now the Oilers would have to face their bitter rivals once more. And the game would be played in Pittsburgh, where the weather in January can be likened to that in the Arctic.

The Oilers were now the Cinderella team of the playoffs. Pittsburgh knew it would have its hands full, and the Steeler defense knew it would have to stop Earl.

"Campbell is just a great running back, just awesome," said Steeler All-Pro linebacker Jack Ham. "You've got to get help if you want to stop him. You've got to get people to the football when he's carrying it. You can't arm-tackle him, and no one man can bring him down, not with his great leg strength and that speed.

"You saw what he did to New England. He ripped them. That's the problem against Houston. You know Campbell's gonna get his yardage, no question about it, but you can't let him run free all day."

As usual, the game promised to be a war. And the day before, the forecast for Pittsburgh was heavy rain. That did not auger well for the Oilers, but Earl seemed unconcerned.

"I played in the rain quite a bit in college," he said. "I played in one game in the ice and snow in high school. So I don't think it will play too much of a factor."

Earl also took time that day to talk about his first year in the pros and what he had learned.

"When I won the Heisman," he said, "I failed to realize so many people would be wanting so much of my attention. So, in a sense, I feel I'm paying a price for it. Some people try to tell you how to run your personal business. There'll be a lot of stuff they'll be trying to tell you to knock you off your peak, break your concentration about some things.

"But it hasn't changed me. I live, and I live happily. I understand very well about the people who hang around. I can count my friends on my fingers.

"I can remember the day I came to the Oilers' camp and found out pro football players are no different from anybody else. They're human beings. But I had some doubts about how my teammates would accept me.

"But now I attribute my success mainly to the talent the Supreme Being gave to me. Secondly, there's my family. And thirdly, the people I've had the opportunity to work with have been good. And finally, it's because I work really hard at it myself."

As usual, Earl was being very honest about everything. He knew he was blessed with great talent, but ever since he had decided to dedicate himself his senior year in high school, he had worked to develop that talent to the utmost. Lesser men with equal talent would not match Earl's achievement.

Now if the Oilers could just win one more game. But when they came out on the field that day it was worse than anyone had imagined. The artificial carpet at Three Rivers Stadium was like a lake. The rain was falling in driving sheets and it was cold and raw.

The weather made the game a travesty, with the football often appearing more like a live greased pig than an oblong pigskin. Unfortunately, the Steelers didn't begin making mistakes until they had left the Oilers swimming for shore.

It was the Steelers right from the opening kick-off. Just five minutes into the game they completed a 57-yard drive in five plays, with the key a 34-yard pass from Terry Bradshaw to Lynn Swann. Franco Harris scored from the seven and the kick made it 7-0. Then late in the period Earl fumbled deep in his own territory and Jack Ham recovered. Two plays later Rocky Bleier ran it in from the 15 and the kick made it 14-0.

Early in the second period Harris returned the favor by fumbling and Robert Brazile recovered it at the Pittsburgh 19. But the Oilers couldn't put it across and had to settle for a 19-yard field goal, making it a 14-3 game. It stayed that way until the final minute of the first half. Then the roof fell in.

At the 14:08 mark the Steelers finished off a 69-yard drive with Bradshaw hitting Swann from 29 yards out. The kick made it 21-3. Houston then fumbled the kickoff and the Steelers recovered. Two plays later, at 14:27, Bradshaw hit John Stallworth in the end zone from the 17. The kick made it 28-3.

The next kickoff wasn't fumbled, but the first Houston play from scrimmage was. Pittsburgh got it again and at 14:56, Roy Gerela booted a 37-yard field goal to make it 31-3. The Steelers had scored 17 points in 48 seconds to all but nail the lid on the Oiler coffin.

In the second half the field was even worse, and the game deteriorated into a comedy of errors. Gerela hit a 22-yard field goal in the third period, and Houston finally got a safety in the same session, making it 34-5. The fourth period was scoreless, and the game and season were over for the Oilers.

It had been a total disaster. The Steelers recovered four of six Houston fumbles, and Earl himself had lost the ball three times. Pastorini, also having his problems in the foul weather, was intercepted five times by the alert Pittsburgh defense. The Steelers also fumbled six times, losing three, but by then the game was out of reach.

"Every time we got something going we committed one of those damn mistakes," Earl complained. He had wound up with 62 yards on 22 carries, still the leading rusher in the game despite everything.

After it was over many of the Oilers accused the Steelers of being cheap-shot artists. Safety Mike Wagner had put Oiler tight end Mike Barber out of the game on what looked to many like an unnecessary hit. And there was some other heavy hitting.

But Earl wouldn't make any accusations. He said the Steelers deserved the victory and had played cleanly, and he admitted he'd be rooting for them to go all the way.

When the team arrived back in Houston they were stunned to find some 40,000 cheering fans waiting for them at the Astrodome. It was a great show of support for a team that had finally come of age. As quarterback Pastorini said:

"Looking at this crowd, I feel like we just won the Super Bowl."

That could very well be in the future for the Oilers, especially now that they have Earl Campbell. As expected, Earl took home a slew of honors after the season. He was everybody's Rookie of the Year, a consensus All-Pro selection as well as the Associated Press Player of the Year. He won a $10,000 prize as Seagram's 7 Crown National Football League MVP. He also won the Bob Hope Great American Youth Award and the Field Scovell Award by the Texas Sports Writers Association for Excellence in Athletic Vigor, Integrity, and Achievement. Those were just a few of them.

He was probably one of the few superstar players ever to go through a year without making a single enemy, without having a hostile word said against him. He was a consummate team player who never hogged the spotlight, who always gave full credit to those around him.

That sentiment was echoed by Earl's running mate, Tim Wilson, who said:

"There are guys who have worked just as hard as Earl who might be upset by the attention he gets and for that reason, the seeds of jealousy are there.

But Earl is the kind of guy who keeps it down just by his very nature. He looks out for the little guy and his positive personality has helped keep the team together."

The question was, could they be together enough on the field to overtake the Steelers as AFC Central champions, and could they make that crucial breakthrough in the playoffs. The team was solid now, and they did have Earl. In fact, once again the question arose as to whether they were using him too much. He had more than 300 carries his rookie year, and they were tough carries, many of them. Wide receiver Ken Burrough was one of the concerned players.

"It would be crazy for Earl to keep carrying the ball so much," Burrough said. "Why have a great Earl Campbell for two years when we can have him for twelve years?"

Trainer Jerry Meins put it this way: "Earl does have an injury potential because of the way he runs He often tends to pull and drag people along with him, and that's a strain."

But Earl didn't want to hear any of that talk. As far as he was concerned, the issue was a closed one.

"I can never change my style," he said, flat out. "I'm going to play the way I've always played. I just love to carry the ball."

Earl was true to his word in the opening game of the 1979 season. The Oilers were at Washington and it was a wild one from the start. The lead changed hands several times, and the Oilers were going to Earl time and again. Early in the final session Washington had a 27-13 lead, but a Pastorini to Billy Johnson pass made it 27-19. A field goal cut it to 27-22, and late in the game it was Earl, cracking over from the three with the winning score. Houston had won its opener, 29-27, and Earl took up where he left off with 166 yards on 32 carries. Not exactly a reduced workload at that.

The next week the team hit a stone wall. . . or better yet, a Steel Curtain. It was the Steelers again, and they whipped the Oilers badly, 38-7, once again holding Earl to less than 100 yards. But the club bounced back, taking Kansas City and Cincy, as Earl ran for 131 and 158 yards and again carried more than 30 times a game.

After a win over Cleveland, the club was upset by St. Louis, then whipped Baltimore with Earl churning out 149 yards on 22 carries. A loss to Seattle left the club with a disappointing 5-3 record for the first half of the season. They had to pick up the pace if they wanted to take the division.

They opened the second half with a 27-24 overtime win against the Jets. They they beat Miami, 9-6, with Earl getting 120 yards. He got 107 in a big, 31-17, victory over Oakland, and 112 in a 42-19 win against Cincinnati. Now the club was 9-3 and battling the Steelers for the division lead. Next came a big one with Dallas, a game billed as the pro championship of Texas.

The game was played before more than 65,000 fans in Dallas' Texas Stadium and in front of a national television audience. The theme was set early. The game was only about two minutes old when the Cowboys' Roger Staubach passed 56-yards to Drew Pearson for a score. Two minutes later, the Oilers were at their own 39 and Pastorini gave the ball to Earl.

With his usual explosive burst, he was through the line and cutting to the outside. The Cowboys are a good pursuit team, but Earl simply turned on the speed and outran them all, going 61 yards for the score. "A brilliant, awesome run," was the way Dallas coach Tom Landry described it.

Late in the second period the Cowboys had moved out to an 11 point lead. Houston drove to the Dallas 27, and Earl got the ball again. This time he burst off left tackle, powered past several prospective tacklers, and drove all the way to the end zone for another big score. By halftime, he had run for 124 yards.

Midway through the final session, Dallas had a 24-23 lead, but Houston had the ball. On a fourth-and -four play, the Oilers decided to play safe and punt. But Dallas was penalized for having too many men on the field. It gave Houston a first down at the Cowboy 32. On the next play Pastorini passed to Burrough for the winning score, as Earl's running helped eat the clock the rest of the way.

The win gave Houston a 10-3 record and a half game lead over Pittsburgh. And Earl Campbell had again made headlines by gaining 195 yards on 33 carries against one of the best defenses in the game.

"Earl is definitely an improved player this year," said backfield coach Andy Bourgeois. "When he came here he used to hit the line as quickly as he could. He's had to learn to slow down and let his offensive line get into its fix so he has more time to see the play develop."

Guard George Reihner explained how the change was made. "The line went through drills with Earl to slow him down," Reihner said. "Last year there would be plays when he was actually out in front of the blocking. Our other backs would read the blocking better than he would. But he got much better as the season wore on, and he's even better this year."

The Dallas game was Earl's fourth, 100-yard game in a row. He was on a real roll. He got 108 in a loss to Cleveland, then finally went over the century mark against the Steelers, running for 109 on 33 tough carries as the Oilers beat Pittsburgh, 20-17. But just when it looked as if they had the division in their grasp, they lost to Philadelphia the final week, 26-20, as Earl got 131 on only 16 carries.

So the club finished at 11-5, a game behind the Steelers, but they made the playoffs as a wildcard team once again. As for Earl, he was more brilliant than ever. He led the NFL in rushing for the second time, this time, getting 1,697 yards on 368 carries, good for a 4.6 average. And he led everyone with 19 big touchdowns. He had lugged the ball some 66 times more than his rookie year and still finished the season strong. Perhaps he was the kind of player who thrived on work after all.

There were more words of praise all around. Oiler assistent general manager Pat Peppler really summed it up when he said that Earl had a blend of talents that made Gale Sayers, Jim Brown, and Jim Taylor all great runners.

"Sayers had the ability to run very low to the ground without going into a duck waddle," said Peppler. "Earl has that same low style of running, but he uses it for power as well as flexibility in cutting. He has the same kind of speed that Brown had and like Taylor, he isn't afraid to hit people. But often he makes a good decision to be elusive and uses his low center of gravity to keep his balance and cut to the outside."

Unfortunately, for Earl and the Oilers, the

playoffs proved very strange and frustrating. First, they had to play the wildcard game against Denver. The Broncos had a 7-3 lead at the end of one, but Earl, who was playing well, culminated a drive with a three-yard run in the second period. Unfortunately, on that run he suffered a groin pull and had to leave. Before that, top receiver Burrough had hurt his back, and then in the third period quarterback Pastorini also went down with a groin pull. The team's three biggest offensive stars were suddenly out of the game and hurt.

Somehow, the Oilers defense rallied to the fore and the club held on for a 13-7 victory. But they had to play the high scoring San Diego Chargers the next week and all three stars were extremely doubtful.

Again, the team compensated and made it. With Earl and Pastorini out, and Burrough only making a token appearance, the Oilers still managed to whip the Chargers, 17-14, as sub QB Gifford Neilson hit Mike Renfro on a 47-yard TD play to win it, while safety Vernon Perry intercepted four Dan Fouts passes and blocked a field goal. The team was sky high, but now had to once again face the Steelers for the AFC championship.

Earl and Pastorini were back and the Oilers made a game of it. They trailed by just 17-10 at the half, and felt they were robbed of a touchdown on a controversial call late in the third. After that, Pittsburgh dominated again and won, 27-13.

As for Earl, he claimed the groin injury didn't slow him. But, it must have, for he had the worst game of his career, gaining just 15 yards on 17 carries. He was stopped behind the line of scrimmage five times, and on another five carries gained only one yard. The Steelers claimed it was their defense, but even an army couldn't hold a healthy Earl Campbell to 15 yards. Yet Earl refused to make excuses.

So another year was ended and still no cigar. Earl received more post-season honors, then got a real surprise. The Oilers decided to renegotiate his original contract. The new pact was reported to be worth some $3 million over a period of six years. That would make Earl one of the highest paid players in the game.

But the problem remained. How to get past the Steelers? Coach Phillips had made the fans a promise. In 1978, he said they knocked at the door. The next year, they were banging on the door, and this coming season, he said, they would kick the door in. Then came another surprise. The team announced it had traded long-time quarterback Dan Pastorini to the Oakland Raiders for their cagey veteran signalcaller, Ken Stabler.

Pastorini had come under criticism for years, the main one being he was bomb happy and would only throw long, often in the wrong situation. Stabler, on the other hand, was a brilliant short and medium-range passer, with the highest completion percentage in league history, around 60 percent. He also knew how to move a team, work the clock, and was an acknowledged winner. It was hoped he'd be the ingredient to put the club over the top.

On the other hand, Kenny was 34 years old and according to some, beginning to slip. So it was a gamble with perhaps Coach Phillips' job on the line if Houston didn't go all the way to the Super Bowl. But it was hoped Stabler would give the

Oilers a more diversified offense, keep all the receivers happy, and maybe use Earl more as a receiver and a little less as a runner.

The 1980 opener put it all on the line right away. You guessed it, the Steelers. The Oilers must have been trying their new offensive philosophy. Stabler threw a lot, 43 times, many of them short and medium passes, and Earl carried just 13 times for 57 yards. He did catch four more for 24, but the result of it all was that the Steelers won easily, 31-17. And some of the Pittsburgh players were surprised that Earl had been used to little.

"No, they can't win like that," said star tackle Mean Joe Greene. "When you've got a howitzer, you've got to fire it."

Another defensive lineman, John Banaszak, added: "I was in shock. In the first half, I had just one running play against me and that was a draw. For the life of me, I can't understand why. The only time they've beat us is when Earl's run 30 times. It freaked me out."

Stabler had played well and there were a number of dropped passes, but the pressure was already on. And the next one wasn't easy, a Monday nighter against another division rival, Cleveland. This time the defense dominated, holding the Browns to seven points, as Earl chugged for 108 on just 18 carries and Stabler completed 23 of 28 passes. Houston won, 16-7, and were in the win column.

They whipped the Colts the next week, 21-16, but Earl hurt a leg and left the game after just seven carries for 11 yards. With Earl on the shelf the next week they got by Cincinnati, 13-10. He returned against Seattle, but was pretty much negated by an early Seahawks lead. The Oilers made a host of mistakes and were soundly beaten, 26-7. The club was at 3-2, and Earl's name was nowhere to be found among the AFC leading rushers. He had just 50 yards on 12 tries against the Seahawks. Some people were already clamouring for Houston to go back to their old success formula and turn Earl loose.

So against Kansas City, Earl got the ball a club record 38 times and ran for 178 yards. But the club faltered again. Stabler wasn't producing big numbers and there were whispers that his arm was shot, that he couldn't throw long if he wanted to. Kansas City quarterback Steve Fuller ran 38 yards for a score with less than three minutes left to give K.C. a 21-20 victory and drop the Oilers back to 3-3.

Then the next week they put it all back in Earl's hands. Against Tampa Bay, a strong defensive team, he ran 33 times and gained a career-high 203 yards, allowing Houston to control the ball for more than 39 minutes. Earl's rampage enabled Stabler to throw to 242 yards and the Oilers won it, 20-14. And fittingly, Earl was back atop the AFC rushers with 605 yards in seven games, though he still trailed rookie Billy Sims of Detroit and the great Walter Payton of the Bears in the NFL race.

The Oilers had made another change. They acquired all-pro tight end Dave Casper from Oakland for a few draft picks, reuniting him with Stabler, and enabling them to run a two tight-end offense with their own star, Mike Barber. Phillips was hoping the move would help, giving his quarterback another short and medium-range target. And there was no denying that Casper was one of the best in the business.

But the key was still Campbell. He showed it again the next week against Cincinnati, carrying 27 times for 202 yards in a 23-3 victory. He became just the second man in NFL history to achieve back-to-back, 200-yard games. The other was O.J. Simpson. Included in this performance was a brilliant, 55-yard TD run.

"Earl plays a whole lot better than I can talk," said Coach Phillips, afterward. "I've run out of words. There just ain't nothin' more I can say about the man."

Earl, as usual, gave credit to his offensive line, calling them "those golden stars in front of me." But it was quarterback Stabler who sounded a warning.

"When you've got a good horse, you've got to ride him," he said, "but you can't ride him to death. I don't fear Earl getting hurt, because he's physically built for punishment. But that doesn't mean he has to be beaten to death.

The whole idea at the beginning was to run Earl less. But suddenly he was running more than ever and the team was tied with Cleveland at 5-3 for the division lead, the Steelers a game back.

With the football world watching to see if Earl could be the first to get 200 yards three straight times, the Oilers went up against Denver. It was a tough game and the Oilers had to come from behind to win, 20-16. Earl carried 36 more times, but gained only 157 yards. *Only?* What other runner in the league would get *only* 157 yards? But Earl was now atop the league's rushers with 964 yards in nine games, and 740 of them in his last four. He was on fire.

Then came a big one with powerful New England and the Oilers showed their grit. They led 24-6 at the half, but allowed the Patriots back in it. Instead of folding up the tent, they got two more scores in the final session and hung on to win, 38-34. Earl scored twice and picked up another 130 yards on 30 carries, while Stabler pitched for 258 yards on beautiful, 15 of 17, pinpoint passing. The Oiler attack seemed in high gear, though 30 carries a game, which now seemed Earl's norm, was a lot.

But he was showing no signs of tiring. Against the Bears the following week he produced his third, 200-yard game, as Houston won, 10-6. And he did it with a dramatic, 48-yard run in the final minute, giving him 206 yards on 31 carries. His performance tied another record for 200-yard days in a season, gave the Oilers the lead in the AFC Central at 8-3, and brought Earl's season rushing total to 1,300 after 11 games.

"The man is incredible," wrote one reporter. "He's been pounding away like this for almost three seasons and seems quicker, stronger, and eager to get the ball again. He could be the best ever."

Still, he always got up slowly and looked as if he couldn't carry one more time.

"Heck, if he goes back to huddle, you know he's all right," said Coach Phillips. "It's when he heads for the sidelines that you've got to start worrying."

A week later the New York Jets surprised the Oilers, getting a 21-0 lead at half. Playing catchup, Earl carried just 15 times for sixty yards as the team made it close, but lost in overtime, 31-28. Stabler had 33 of 51 for a career-high 388 yards. One reason Earl didn't carry more was that he bruised a thigh in the third quarter and left the game.

He bounced back to gain 109 against Cleveland, but the tough Browns won a 17-14 decision, making the Houston record 8-5, and leaving them a game behind Cleveland and tied with Pittsburgh. Then came a strange showdown game with the Steelers. The two defenses totally dominated the action and only a pair of Toni Fritsch field goals in the second half lit up the board. Houston won 6-0, the first time the Steelers were blanked in 114 games, and Earl had 81 of the toughest yards he ever got in his life.

The final two games of the regular season showed just how great Earl Campbell had become. Against Green Bay he toted 36 times for 181 yards in a 22-3 victory. Then in the finale against Minnesota, he carried 29 more times and was as unstoppable as he'd been all year long. He got 203 yards, to set a new record for 200-yard games, as the Oilers clinched a wildcard berth with a 20-16 victory. They finished the year at 11-5, tied with Cleveland, but the Browns were given the divisional crown because of a better record within the division.

But what an incredible year it had been for Earl Campbell. He led the NFL in rushing for a third straight year, gaining 1,934 yards, just 69 short of O.J. Simpson's record of 2,003. And if he hadn't missed some seven quarters of action early in the year he might have broken it. He also carried a career-high 373 times and still had a 5.2 yard per carry average.

In three short years, he had gone over the 5,000 yard mark, with 5,081 yards. In fact, he was now averaging some 1,693 yards a season, on an average of 347 carries a year, and his per rush average for his career was nearly 4.9 yards a crack. When told about all this, Earl was almost matter-of-fact.

"Next year," he said, "I'll work even harder in the off season. Then I'll shoot for O.J.'s record."

He also added: "My offensive line did the job all year, as they always do, and Tim Wilson has been an incredible blocking back. Some days he's like my eyes. He hits the holes for me and I just follow him through."

Wilson answered the praise. "Earl has something I've never seen in a running back. He has the ability to keep going when it looks like he's down and out and doesn't have anything left. Somehow he finds more."

He had to find some more before the year ended. The Oilers had to play a wildcard game against the very tough and physical Oakland Raiders. And again their fans asked if this would be the year the Oilers broke through?

The Raiders opened the scoring with a field goal, but before the quarter ended, the Oilers drove downfield and Earl bulled his way over from the one, giving Houston a 7-3 lead. The Raiders got the only score in the second period, making it 10-7, as their defense swarmed around Earl, making the yards very tough ones. And when the third period remained scoreless, the game was still up for grabs with just 15 minutes left.

But then the Raiders took command. First halfback Arthur Whittington took a 44-yard TD pass from Jim Plunkett. Then Chris Bahr kicked a 37-yard field goal, and finally, Lester Hayes intercepted a Stabler pass and ran it in from 20 yards out. Oakland won it, 27-7, and the Oilers were out of it again.

Earl had gained 91 yards on 27 tough carries,

good for only a 3.4 average, which showed that the Raider defense was keying on him. And after it ended, some of the Houston players publically criticized the coaching staff.

"We have good talent, but no direction," said linebacker Greg Bingham, for one. "We need some coaching changes. There's no reason we couldn't have scored more than seven points in a game like this."

Phillips admitted, "We were outplayed and out-coached. The Raiders played as well as any team I've seen in the 12 years I've been in pro ball."

The Oakland win was no fluke. The Raiders went on to win the Super Bowl, becoming the first wild card team to do so. But many of the Oilers still felt they were good enough to be there and that changes would have to be made. Shortly after the season ended, there was a change. Bum Phillips was fired as coach and no one took it harder than Earl. One source close to the team said that Earl and Bum had a father-son relationship.

"Earl is taking this very hard," the source said. "Bum did a lot for Earl and they grew real close. It became a father-son relationship and now it's been broken up. Earl is confused, angry, and resentful. He played his heart out for Bum this past year, took a lot of punishment, yet ignored the pain."

There seemed to be a lot of truth in that, for shortly after Phillips' firing, Earl's agent said that his client wanted yet another new contract, one calling for some $1 million per season. Otherwise, Earl would sit out the season. So far, the Oilers have refused and the impasse continues.

It's difficult to see Earl sitting out and it's equal-ly difficult to see the Oilers allowing their best player, their big gun, to get away or remain unhappy. It seems that something will be worked out before the 1981 season begins.

When you look back over the record, it's hard to believe what Earl Campbell has accomplished in three pro seasons. First there were his origins, being crowded into that weatherbeaten house in Tyler with 10 brothers and sisters. But he stepped forward and has made his dreams come true. Still, when he thinks of the future, it is always back in Tyler, living on the land he has bought there for his family.

"I'd love to run a summer football camp there someday," he has said. "Maybe even teach the kids how to milk cows and ride horses. And at night, we can sit around a fire and talk about their problems."

Sound far fetched. Not with Earl. He's a man who has learned how to achieve his goals. In fact, there are many NFL defensive players who wouldn't mind seeing Earl run that camp right now, fulltime. They would even send their own kids there if it kept Earl off the gridiron and they no longer had to tackle the human battering-ram that comes at them every year.

But Earl's football future is still unlimited, as is his future as a human being. The Tyler Rose will undoubtedly continue to bloom for a long time to come.

LONG GAINERS — STATISTICS

Earl Campbell

Team	Year	Att.	Yards	Average	TD
Texas	1974	162	928	5.7	6
Texas	1975	198	1,118	5.6	13
Texas	1976	138	653	4.7	3
Texas	1977	267	1,744	6.5	19
College Totals		765	4,443	5.8	41
Houston	1978	302	1,450	4.8	13
Houston	1979	368	1,697	4.6	19
Houston	1980	373	1,934	5.2	13
Pro Totals		1,043	5,081	4.9	45

Billy Sims

Team	Year	Att.	Yards	Average	TD
Oklahoma	1975	15	95	6.3	2
Oklahoma	1976	3	44	-14.6	0
Oklahoma	1977	65	406	6.2	6
Oklahoma	1978	231	1,762	7.6	20
Oklahoma	1979	224	1,506	6.7	22
College Totals		538	3,813	7.09	50
Detroit	1980	313	1,303	4.2	16
Pro Totals		313	1,303	4.2	16

Team	Year	No.	Yards	Average	TD
		John Jefferson			
Arizona State	1974	30	423	14.1	1
Arizona State	1975	44	808	18.4	5
Arizona State	1976	48	681	14.2	5
Arizona State	1977	53	912	17.2	8
College Totals		175	2,824	16.1	19
San Diego	1978	56	1,001	17.9	13
San Diego	1979	61	1,090	17.9	10
San Diego	1980	82	1,340	16.3	13
Pro Totals		199	3,431	17.2	36
		Russ Francis			
Oregon	1972	8	93	11.6	0
Oregon	1973	31	495	16.0	4
College Totals		39	588	15.1	4
New England	1975	35	636	18.2	4
New England	1976	26	367	14.1	3
New England	1977	16	229	14.3	4
New England	1978	39	543	13.9	4
New England	1979	39	557	14.3	5
New England	1980	41	664	16.2	8
Pro Totals		196	2,996	15.3	28